The Story of the Choctaw Indians

THE STORY OF THE CHOCTAW INDIANS

❖

From the Past to the Present

Joe E. Watkins

The Story of the American Indian

 GREENWOOD™

An Imprint of ABC-CLIO, LLC
Santa Barbara, California • Denver, Colorado

Library of Congress Cataloging-in-Publication Data

Names: Watkins, Joe, 1951– author.
Title: The story of the Choctaw Indians : from the past to the present /
    Joe E. Watkins.
Description: Santa Barbara, California : Greenwood, an imprint of ABC-CLIO,
    2019. | Series: The story of the American Indian | Includes
    bibliographical references and index.
Identifiers: LCCN 2018035765 (print) | LCCN 2018036364 (ebook) |
    ISBN 9781440862670 (ebook) | ISBN 9781440862663 (hard copy : alk. paper)
Subjects: LCSH: Choctaw Indians—History—Juvenile literature.
Classification: LCC E99.C8 (ebook) | LCC E99.C8 W38 2019 (print) |
    DDC 976.004/97387—dc23
LC record available at https://lccn.loc.gov/2018035765

ISBN: 978-1-4408-6266-3 (print)
        978-1-4408-6267-0 (ebook)

23 22 21 20 19   1 2 3 4 5

This book is also available as an eBook.

Greenwood
An Imprint of ABC-CLIO, LLC

ABC-CLIO, LLC
130 Cremona Drive, P.O. Box 1911
Santa Barbara, California 93116-1911
www.abc-clio.com

This book is printed on acid-free paper ∞

Manufactured in the United States of America

Contents

Series Foreword

Historical Native Americans find a place in history books, but often as relics of the past. Exploring American Indian history and learning about their struggles, contributions, and cultures, both in the past and present, is vital to truly understand the American story. American Indians and Alaska Natives have a long and varied history and continue on as vibrant, contemporary peoples comprising more than 6.6 million people living in the United States.

Of the 573 federally recognized American Indian tribes, each has its own history and complex relationship with the United States. *The Story of the American Indian* explores the diverse and wide range of American Indian peoples. Books in the series focus on the histories of individual tribes and encourage readers to break down stereotypes and resist the urge to lump all indigenous people into one group. Unlike many reference books on Native Americans, books in this series share histories from tribal perspectives rather than from traditional colonizers' viewpoints. Authors are tribal members and scholars who have extensive firsthand knowledge of their tribe.

Each volume focuses on a particular group or related groups of American Indians and presents historical chapters about the events, homelands, language, and community; cultural and social traditions; contributions to the larger society; and the tribe's current status. Volumes include a timeline of historical events, chronological narrative chapters, brief biographies in a Notable People section, and a bibliography. These richly detailed books provide readers with a holistic picture of the tribe from the past to the present.

Preface

It is difficult to adequately describe "The Choctaw"* without taking into consideration the complex histories of the three federally recognized tribal groups—the Choctaw Nation of Oklahoma, the Mississippi Band of Choctaw Indians, and the Jena Band of Choctaw Indians. Although each of the three tribes is a distinct political and social entity, they all shared common histories until 1832, when the first groups of Choctaw migrated from their homelands in Mississippi to Indian Territory. The marches to Indian Territory split up the Choctaw socially, physically, and economically. Those who survived the treks westward established a new government in a new place and eventually became the Choctaw Nation of Oklahoma. Those who chose to stay in central Mississippi created a distinct social group that is now known as the Mississippi Band of Choctaw Indians. The history of the Jena Band of Choctaw Indians is rooted in families who chose to wander westward into Louisiana and Texas, and is much less documented prior to the 1880s.

---

* A note on names and naming: More frequent usage of the tribal name is *Choctaw*, although, among tribal members and occasionally within tribal documents, the word *Chahta* or *Chata* may be used. In some of the origin stories that follow, *Chata* is used to portray the name of one of the mythical brothers who led the migration to the ancestral land; *Chahta* is often encountered in other stories as well.

Historically, the Choctaw were actually a series of villages spread across Alabama, Mississippi, southern Tennessee, and Louisiana. Each town had a leader—someone who could be considered a "chief" by the Europeans, even though the individuals only spoke for the people who lived within the widely dispersed homes within their regional sphere of influence. Only after becoming integrated into the broader U.S. history and economy did the Choctaw adopt the European concept of a centrally recognized political leader.

The Choctaw entered into treaties with European countries as early as 1738, when Great Britain entreated with the Tribe in the Treaty of Charleston for "Trade and Alliance." The first between the United States and the Choctaw Nation was the Treaty of Hopewell in 1786, which served to define the boundaries of the Choctaw and to provide notice that the United States was to act as protectorate of the Tribe. But the treaty with the most far-reaching impact on the Tribe (at the time and into the future) was the 1830 Treaty of Dancing Rabbit Creek, which called for removal of tribal members to Indian Territory and granted U.S. citizenship to those who decided to give up their tribal membership and remain in Mississippi.

With removal came separation: those who moved to Indian Territory in the three waves of 1831, 1832, and 1833 settled into the southeastern portion of Indian Territory (now Oklahoma) and established a government system that has survived allotment and termination to become what is now known as the Choctaw Nation of Oklahoma. Those who chose to remain in Mississippi survived as state citizens until regaining recognition as the Mississippi Band of Choctaw Indians on April 20, 1945, under the Indian Reorganization Act of 1934. The first evidence of a Choctaw habitation in the vicinity of Jena (Catahoula Parish), Louisiana, is an 1880 census listing 26 Indians; by 1890, the count had grown to 34; the Tribe received acknowledgement as a federally recognized tribe in 1995.

Telling the story of these three distinct tribes is difficult, and occasionally unwieldy. All three groups share a general history until the Treaty of Dancing Rabbit Creek. Chapter 1 offers the deep time (archaeological) background that led up to the groups of people encountered by Spaniard Hernando De Soto and his exploration party. Chapter 2 chronicles the interactions between the various European colonizers and the Choctaw, including the American period, ending with the Treaty of Dancing Rabbit Creek and removal. Chapter 3 discusses the impact of the Treaty of Dancing Rabbit Creek and removal, and sets the underlying foundations for the three separate Choctaw Nations that are recognized by the federal government today.

Chapter 4 begins the discussion of the post-removal structures that underlie the three separate groups of Choctaw Indians. It discusses the period from the early 1830s up to the early twentieth century. Chapter 5 discusses the time period from the early twentieth century at the end of the allotment period, discussing the impact of various federal government policies of allotment, attempted termination of the Oklahoma Choctaws and the reorganization of the Mississippi Band of Choctaw Indians, and conflicting governmental policies of termination to self-determination and self-sufficiency; it concludes with a discussion of the recognition of the Jena Band of Choctaw Indians in Louisiana.

Chapter 6 provides an overview of the contemporary groups that make up the three federally recognized tribes of Choctaw Indians—the Choctaw Nation of Oklahoma, the Mississippi Band of Choctaw Indians, and the Jena Band of Choctaw Indians in Louisiana. It also provides information on some of the nonfederally recognized groups of Choctaw Indians.

Acknowledgments

As always, I thank my wife, Carol Ellick, for her support through this and other projects. I also wish to acknowledge the work of Choctaw people who have been supportive of me, and my work, especially Ian Thompson, the current tribal historic preservation officer (THPO) of the Choctaw Nation of Oklahoma. I also wish to acknowledge the current and past leadership of the Choctaw Nation of Oklahoma, the Mississippi Band of Choctaw Indians, and the Jena Band of Choctaw Indians, who have worked throughout the good and bad times to keep the Choctaw people moving forward. I hope my son, Ethan, and daughter, Sydney, can gain a better understanding of where their ancestors came from and what they went through to become "Choctaw."

Finally, I acknowledge Parker Rivera, who, when asked about the Choctaw, said "I've never heard of the Choctaw." Hopefully this book will help him and others like him gain a better knowledge of who the Choctaw are, their history, and their bright futures.

Introduction

The Choctaw are actually comprised of three different and distinct con-temporary, federally recognized tribes that share a common Muskogean lan-guage. The three groups have what might be considered a common history up to 1830, even though there were likely regional differences even from the beginning.

Much of the common history of the groups is derived from the deep archaeological past, but the Choctaw tell three stories about how they came into being. One version of the Choctaw origin story goes thus:

> A very long time ago the first creation of people was in Nanih Waiya, and there they were made, and there they came forth. The Musco-gees (Creeks) first came out of Nanih Waiya, and they dried them-selves on Nanih Waiya's earthen rampart, and when they got dry, they went to the east. On this side of the Tombigbee, there they rested, and as they were smoking tobacco, they dropped some fire.
>
> The Cherokees next came out of Nanih Waiya. And they dried themselves on Nanih Waiya's earthen rampart, and when they got dry, they went and followed the trail of the elder tribe. And at the place where the Muscogees had stopped and rested, and where they had smoked tobacco, there was fire and the woods were burnt, and the Cherokees could not find the Muscogees' trail, so they got lost and turned aside and went north, and there, toward the north, they set-tled and made a people.

And the Chickasaws third came out of Nanih Waiya. And they sunned themselves on the earthen rampart, and when they got dry, they went and followed the Cherokees' trail. And when they got to where the Cherokees had settled and made a people, they settled and made a people close to the Cherokees.

And the Choctaws fourth and last came out of Nanih Waiya. And they then sunned themselves on the earthen rampart, and when they got dry, they looked around and saw that this was a perfect place to live. They did not go anywhere, but settled down in this very land, and it is the Choctaws' home.

A second story tells of a great migration led by two brothers, and offers a shared history with the Chickasaw Tribe/Nation (Cushman, 1899; Baird, 1973). Here is a shortened version of this story as presented by Baird (1973):

At the dawn of time, the ancestors of the Choctaw people lived in a land far to the west amongst many other peoples. The ancestors of the Choctaw grew restless and left this land.

Leading them were two brothers, Chata and Chickasa, who were guided by a sacred pole. Each night the brothers would plant the pole in the ground and each morning the pole would be leaning toward the east. So the journey continued eastward through strange lands and across a great river until one morning the pole remained upright.

Those people led by Chata took this as a sign that their journey was at an end while those led by Chickasa continued a little farther and became the Chickasaw people.

To celebrate their arrival the Choctaw people then constructed great earthen mounds, the largest of which is Nanih Waiya.

A third story also tells of the brothers Chata and Chickasa, but adds an element of relations with ancestors to the story. In the third story, the Choctaw had a very difficult time traveling because they were carrying the bones of their deceased with them, often having to make extra trips just to transport all of the remains. According to this account, their connection to their ancestors was so strong that "they would have preferred to die and rot with these bones in the wilderness, sooner than leave them behind" (Lincecum, 1904, reproduced in Swanton, [1931] 2001, p. 12). Pesantubbee (2005) alludes to the fact that the migration took so long because the people traveled for half a day with one-half of the ancestors' bones and then returned for the other half and carried them to the evening's camps. At last, once they settled in their final habitation place, they placed the bones on the ground and constructed the mound over them.

NANIH WAIYA

This large rectangular platform mound, measuring 25 feet high, 218 feet long, and 140 feet wide, is maintained in a state park located northeast of Philadelphia, Mississippi. Nanih Waiya (in Choctaw the words are presented as *Nvnih Waiya* or *Nvnih Waiya*) is a Choctaw Indian name meaning "leaning hill." A small burial mound, now nearly leveled by plowing, is located outside the park boundaries several hundred yards away. A long, raised embankment once enclosed the site. Most of this earthen enclosure has been destroyed by cultivation, but a short segment remains along the edge of a swamp to the northwest of the large mound.

The period of construction of Nanih Waiya Mound is uncertain. Although its rectangular, flat-topped form is typical of Mississippian period mounds (1000 to1600 CE), pottery sherds found on the surface of the adjacent habitation area suggest a possible Middle Woodland time range (100 BCE to 400 CE). By the 18th century, Nanih Waiya came to be venerated by the Choctaw tribe. The site plays a central role in the tribe's origin legends: in one version, the mound gave birth to the tribe, and the people emerged from the underworld here and rested on the mound's slopes to dry before populating the surrounding region.

In Oklahoma, the first capital of the Choctaw Nation in Indian Territory and the earliest seat of government established within Oklahoma is at a location called Nunih Waya (Nanih Waiya), approximately 1.5 miles west of Tuskahoma in present Pushmataha County. On the completion of their removal to Indian Territory, the Choctaw reorganized their government under a new constitution in 1834. They constructed their first council house in 1838 at a site they named Nunih Waya, in honor of the "mother mound" in Mississippi.

These stories form a philosophical basis for the origin of the Choctaw and provide a broad description of the reasoning why the Choctaw came to be in the area where European colonial powers (the Spanish, French, English, and later the Americans) encountered and interacted with them. Still, though the stories are philosophical in nature, they serve to give a brief idea that the land of the Choctaws—whether the original homeland of Nanih Waiya in Mississippi; the homeland of the Choctaw Capitol in Tuskahoma, Oklahoma; or the homeland of the Jena Band of Choctaw Indians in Louisiana—is at the heart of Choctaw identity.

The actual origin of the Choctaw is lost in time, but it is likely that the first people whose descendants became the Choctaw were the Paleoindian group known as "Clovis" who first inhabited what is now known as the southeastern United States about 12,000 years ago. Through time, occupants of the lands in the Southeast developed cultures more reliant on local animals and plants, and also developed technological improvements that contributed to their cultural growth. Through the period known as the Archaic, local groups developed ground stone tools that helped them process plant foods more efficiently, and also developed reliance on local plant and animal communities. In the Woodland period, local communities gathered into more permanent communities and came to rely more heavily on plant foods for their caloric intake. Later in the Woodland, the development of the bow and arrow as hunting and warfare implements represents a major technological hallmark of the period.

At the time of European exploration of the Southeast, the Choctaw were within the declining aspects of what archaeologists have labeled the Mississippian culture—a time of marked social hierarchy and reliance on corn as a staple food, construction and use of large earth works and mounds, and evidence of long-distance trade networks. Many of the Mississippian settlements were abandoned right at the time of European contact, and it has been suggested that much of the unrest at the end of this period was a result of European diseases that struck populations in advance of the actual Europeans themselves.

Spanish conquistadors, led by Hernando De Soto, came into what is now western Alabama in October 1540. De Soto's original intent was to annex the land, take its resources, and enslave its population (Clayton, Knight, & Moore, 1993). Yet, ultimately they came to the view that "it was impossible to rule such bellicose people or to subjugate such bold men . . . it seemed to them that neither by force nor by persuasion could they be brought under the authority and dominion of the Spaniards; they would allow themselves to be killed first" (Garcilaso, [1596] 1993: 356). The Spanish soon left the area, crossing the Mississippi River in 1541 and entering into what is now Arkansas. De Soto died in 1542, but roughly half of the expedition survived to return to Mexico (Elvas, [1557] 1993).

The specific name *Chahta* first appears in European texts and maps during late 1600s (Galloway, 1995). The Choctaw became allies with the French in trading and warfare, whereas the Chickasaw to the north were allied with the English (Pesantubbee, 2005). A dichotomy of alliances within the Tribe was similarly exploited by the European powers to precipitate a disastrous Choctaw Civil War of 1747–1750 while a simultaneous wave of European diseases took even more lives (Adair, 1775).

Following the French defeat in the Seven Years War in 1763, the Choctaw were forced to deal with the English. With the defeat of the English in the Revolutionary War, Choctaw–American relations became paramount. As military allies, the Choctaw helped the new country survive challenges by the English and the French, but relationships with the United States under Andrew Jackson worsened. Ultimately, in 1830, under continual threat of unprovoked military invasion, some Choctaw leaders ceded the last of the homeland in the Treaty of Dancing Rabbit Creek against the wishes of the majority (Claiborne, 1880).

The Choctaw Nation of Oklahoma is composed of those Choctaw who moved to Oklahoma from Mississippi following the Treaty of Dancing Rabbit Creek in 1830. Following removal to the Indian Territory, the Choctaws established their own government under a written constitution in 1834; the constitution was modified in 1837 to include the Chickasaw; however, the Chickasaw became a separate nation again in 1855.

Following the Civil War, the Choctaw were forced to sell their Western lands as punishment for having sided with the Confederacy. A new constitution established a government modeled explicitly on the American model, but the incursion of many non-Indians in the Choctaw lands compounded the situation. By far the most damaging aspect of U.S. policy toward the Choctaw came as a result of the Dawes Severalty Commission's actions to allot tribal land to individual Indian citizens. Under the Atoka Agreement of 1897, the Choctaw agreed to allotment, with the "surplus" lands opened up to non-Indian habitation. In 1906, allotment for tribal members was closed, and in 1907, the Choctaws were absorbed into the new state of Oklahoma.

The 1934 Indian Reorganization Act allowed the Oklahoma Choctaw to elect an advisory council, and in 1948, they elected their own principle chief. Escaping Termination proved to be a complex task, with some seeing it as a panacea to individual Choctaw economic woes, but urban Choctaws organized to prevent termination (Lambert, 2007a). In 1978, the Tribe adopted a new constitution that created a tribal council form of government led by a principal chief elected by popular vote of the entire nation. Council members were elected by popular vote of council districts.

The Choctaw Nation of Oklahoma, with tribal offices in Durant, Oklahoma, is largest of the three contemporary tribes of Choctaws. The Tribe's membership was listed as 190,436 as of December 18, 2017, with 247,757 Choctaws listed as having a Certificate of Degree of Indian Blood (CDIB). A much smaller number actually live in the 11-county jurisdictional area of southeastern Oklahoma, but other areas of large Choctaw population include cities and towns of Oklahoma, California, Texas, and other cities where Choctaw were transplanted in the 1950s by the federal relocation plan.

In Mississippi, the Choctaw tribal members who had remained were largely ignored. Choctaws primarily stayed in the background in the racialized South of Mississippi, choosing to quietly maintain their Indian culture and language. The establishment of the Choctaw Indian Agency in Philadelphia, Mississippi, in 1918 brought their plight back into notice, and by 1944, more than 16,000 acres had been purchased for tribal members. In 1945, the U.S. Secretary of the Interior granted the Choctaws formal recognition as an Indian tribe, approving a constitution and bylaws for the Mississippi Band of Choctaw Indians. The constitution allowed for a tribal chairman to be appointed by an elected tribal council, and the land that had been acquired for them became the Band's reservation.

The Mississippi Band of Choctaw Indians continued to struggle in the South during their initial years of recognition, but the passage of the Indian Self-Determination and Education Assistance Act of 1975 authorized the Tribe to take over the management of government programs, and economic development initiatives replaced abject poverty on the reservation, creating job opportunities for tribal members and nontribal members alike. The Band's membership was listed as 5,190 people in the 2000 census, but the Band's website notes it is "about 10,000" (Mississippi Band of Choctaw Indians, 2015).

The Jena Band of Choctaw Indians is perhaps the least known of the three Choctaw groups and is derived from Choctaws who moved westward from the Mississippi homelands in the early 1800s. A small community was noted near present-day Jena, Louisiana, in the 1880s. In 1903, most of these people were identified by the Dawes Commission as being eligible to receive allotments in the Choctaw Nation of Oklahoma. Some of the community members moved to Oklahoma, but others remained in Louisiana.

The local officials near Jena created a school for the Choctaw kids in 1932, but the school lost federal funding and was closed in 1938. In 1974, the group created a formal nonprofit group known as The Jena Band of Choctaw Indians of Louisiana, and the Louisiana legislature passed a resolution that formally recognized the Choctaw Indian community at Jena as an Indian tribe. The Jena Band of Choctaw Indians received federal recognition through the federal acknowledgment process in 1995. Their tribal membership was listed as 327 on the 2015 edition of the tribal website (Jena Band of Choctaw Indians, 2015).

So it is that there are three separate and distinct Choctaw entities, each with an intertwined history until about 1830, when removal and relocation as a result of the Treaty of Dancing Rabbit Creek created the schism. Those who moved to Oklahoma established a tribal government that dealt with the United States on a government-to-government basis until the Confederacy lost the Civil War. The people of Choctaw descent who remained in Mississippi lived under the jurisdiction of the state of Mississippi until regaining tribal standing in 1945. The group of people who had moved to the Jena area maintained their own tribal community but was required to go through the federal recognition processes to regain standing as a tribe. Thus, these three tribal groups have followed divergent paths to reach their contemporary community structures.

In the following chapters, the reader is presented with information on the larger groups that split into multiple sources. Each tribal group has its own history—sometimes interconnected with the other two, but more often separated from the others. Because so much more has been written about the largest of the three groups, and much less so about the smallest one, the amount of space devoted to each may seem to be weighted more heavily toward the Oklahoma Choctaw than the others. Still, the manuscript provides detail on the three tribes, to prove beneficial to readers everywhere who are interested in learning about the historic trajectories that led to the development of contemporary Choctaw culture.

Timeline

1540
Hernando De Soto, leading his well-equipped Spanish fortune hunters, makes contact with the Choctaws.

1698
Frenchman Pierre Le Moyne, Sieur d'Iberville, leads the initial expedition to establish the colony of Louisiana.

1738
Choctaw and Great Britain enter into the Treaty of Charleston.

1746
Englishman James Adair begins to trade in the Eastern district of Choctaw territory.

1747–1750
The Choctaw engage in a civil war between English and French supporters.

1754–1763
The French and Indian War, culminated in the Peace of Paris, results in the Choctaws becoming a part of the British Empire.

1775–1783
The American Revolution begins a period of new alignments for the Choctaws and other southern Indians.

1786
Choctaws sign the Treaty of Hopewell with the new U.S. government, placing themselves under its protection.

1798, April 7
Congress creates the Territory of Mississippi.

1801
The Fort Adams Treaty is signed, with the Choctaw ceding the southwestern corner of their land and giving the United States the right to construct a road through Choctaw country from Natchez to Nashville, Tennessee.

1802
The Fort Confederation Treaty is signed, with the Choctaw ceding a tract north of Mobile.

1803
Louisiana Territory is transferred to the United States, ending rivalry of foreign powers within the Choctaw nation. President Thomas Jefferson suggests to Congress that Indians be moved west of the Mississippi.

1804
An act organizing the Louisiana Territory is passed, including a provision for giving Western lands to Indians in exchange for their eastern domains.

1805
The Mount Dexter Treaty is signed, resulting in the Choctaw ceding the remaining strip of their southern territory.

1811
Tecumseh visits the Choctaw, urging an Indian Confederation. Pushmataha persuades his people not to arouse the enmity of a stronger and more numerous people.

1812–1815
Further affirming his allegiance to the United States, Pushmataha leads several hundred warriors with Jackson at the Battles of Horseshoe Bend and New Orleans.

1820
The Treaty of Doak's Stand is signed, whereby the Choctaw agree to give up portions of their homeland in exchange for lands in the West to be established in Indian Territory.

1824
Several Chiefs journey to Washington to try to rectify problems in the 1820 treaty. Apukshunubbee dies from a fall in Kentucky; Pushmataha dies from "croup" in Washington City.

1825
The Treaty of Washington City provides options for the Choctaw to stay in Mississippi in addition to financial annuities for the Tribe. It also results in the cession of lands in what was then Arkansas Territory, relinquishment of a Choctaw

debt, and the creation of an agent and blacksmith for the Choctaws west of the Mississippi.

1830
The Indian Removal Act passes Congress.

1830
The Treaty of Dancing Rabbit Creek is signed, with the Choctaw agreeing to give up their eastern lands for lands in Indian Territory.

1832–1834
The Choctaw undertake relocation to Indian Territory.

1834
Choctaw Nation of Oklahoma drafts a new Constitution.

1835
Chief Moshulatubbee dies in Mississippi.

1838
Choctaw Nation of Oklahoma creates new Constitution in Oklahoma.

1847
Choctaw Nation of Oklahoma collects $710 to aid victims of the potato famine in Ireland.

1855
A new Choctaw Constitution for Choctaw Nation of Oklahoma separates Chickasaw from Choctaw.

1860
Choctaw Nation of Oklahoma passes a new constitution.

1861–1865
The Choctaw ally with the South in the Civil War.

1866
Choctaw Nation of Oklahoma negotiates a new treaty with the United States. The Treaty of 1866 requires the Choctaw to give up the western one-third of their land for settlement of more tribes. The treaty also allows north–south and east–west railroads.

1880
Jena Band of Choctaw Indians—U.S. Census mentions 26 Choctaw people living in Catahoula Parish.

1887
Choctaw Nation of Oklahoma—Dawes Act passed Congress, intending to break up tribal lands into individual allotments.

1890
Jena Band of Choctaw Indians—U.S. Census lists 10 families in Catahoula Parish.

1893
Choctaw Nation of Oklahoma—The Dawes Severalty Act is introduced to the Five Civilized Tribes.

1897
Choctaw Nation of Oklahoma—The Atoka Agreement is signed, resulting in allotment of the Choctaw lands in Oklahoma, with "surplus" lands opened up to non-Indian habitation.

1903
Jena Band of Choctaw Indians—The Dawes Commission recognizes some of the Jena Choctaw families as "Mississippi Choctaw."

1906
Choctaw Nation of Oklahoma—The Curtis Act is signed, resulting in the abolition of the Choctaw tribal government, and Choctaw tribal county and district officials cease to function.

1907
Oklahoma becomes the 46th state of the Union.

1910
Mississippi Band of Choctaw Indians—1,253 Choctaws still live in Mississippi.

1913–1919
Choctaw Nation of Oklahoma—The U.S. government tries to liquidate Oklahoma Choctaw timber and mineral resources.

1916
Mississippi Band of Choctaw Indians—An outside investigation of Mississippi Choctaws, initiated by the U.S. Government, reveals a deplorable state.

1918
The Choctaw language is used as a code in World War I by the Choctaw Code Talkers.

Choctaw Nation of Oklahoma—Joseph Oklahombi receives acknowledgment as Oklahoma's Greatest Hero of World War I.

Mississippi Band of Choctaw Indians—The Bureau of Indian Affairs establishes an agency in Philadelphia, Mississippi, to establish schools and assist the Choctaws who had stayed.

1920
Mississippi Band of Choctaw Indians—The Choctaw Land Acquisition Program is begun.

1921
Mississippi Band of Choctaw Indians—Dr. Frank J. McKinley begins serving as the first superintendent of the Choctaw Agency in Philadelphia, Mississippi.

1924

Citizenship granted by Congress to all Indians.

1926

Mississippi Band of Choctaw Indians—A 35-bed hospital is established for the Mississippi Choctaws at Philadelphia. Dr. Robert J. Enochs serves as superintendent to the Choctaw Agency from May 18, 1926, until June 1932.

1932–1938

Mississippi Band of Choctaw Indians—A. C. Hector serves as superintendent to the Choctaw Agency.

Jena Band of Choctaw Indians—The Penick Indian School operates under the leadership of Mattie Penick.

1934

Congress passes the "Indian New Deal," consisting of the Indian Reorganization Act (1934), the Johnson-O'Malley Act (1934), and the Indian Arts and Crafts Board Act (1935) to end allotment and to allow tribes better control of their own affairs.

Mississippi Band of Choctaw Indians—January: First notation occurs of an active 17-member Choctaw Business Committee holding an election.

1935

Mississippi Band of Choctaw Indians—March 30: The Choctaw of Mississippi vote to accept the provisions of the Indian Reorganization Act.

1936

Choctaw Nation of Oklahoma—The Oklahoma Indian Welfare Act is passed, extending the Indian Reorganization Act to include those tribes within the boundary of Oklahoma.

1938

Mississippi Band of Choctaw Indians—Lewis W. Page serves as superintendent to the Choctaw Agency for one month; Harvey K. Meyer replaces him and serves as superintendent until August 1940.

1939

Mississippi Band of Choctaw Indians—June 21: An act authorizing the Secretary of the Interior to declare the lands in trust for the benefit of the Mississippi Choctaws passes Congress.

1940

Mississippi Band of Choctaw Indians—Archie McMullen serves as superintendent to the Choctaw Agency from September until August 1951.

1944

Mississippi Band of Choctaw Indians—May: Van T. Barfoot earns the Congressional Medal of Honor in World War II.

Mississippi Band of Choctaw Indians—August: The proposed Choctaw Constitution is approved.

Mississippi Band of Choctaw Indians—December: 15,150 acres are declared to be an Indian Reservation for the Mississippi Band of Choctaw Indians.

1945

Mississippi Band of Choctaw Indians—Mississippi Choctaw Tribal Council is organized under the act of 1934. The Secretary of the Interior approves the constitution and bylaws of the Mississippi Band of Choctaw Indians. The first regular meeting of the Choctaw Tribal Council is held, and Joe Chitto of the Standing Pine Community is elected as chairman.

1946

Congress creates the Indian Claims Commission.

1948

Choctaw Nation of Oklahoma—Harry J. W. Belvin is appointed as the seventh Choctaw chief of the twentieth century.

1949

Mississippi Band of Choctaw Indians—Emmett York is elected Chairman of the Choctaw Tribal Council.

The first Choctaw Indian Fair is held.

1950–1956

The federal termination policy is given impetus with the statutory termination of several tribes by Congress.

1953

Congress passes the Termination Act to free Indians from federal supervision, abolish the BIA, and allow Native Americans to become "full-fledged" American citizens.

1956

Mississippi Band of Choctaw Indians—Paul Vance is appointed as superintendent of the Choctaw Agency and remains until 1962.

1959

Choctaw Nation of Oklahoma—Congress passes House Resolution 2722, intended to terminate the Choctaw tribe of Oklahoma.

1964

Mississippi Band of Choctaw Indians—The Choctaw Community Action Agency is formed to plan construction of houses, offices, and utilities. Through the Economic Opportunity Act, a grant of $15,000, and assistance from university management experts, the agency is effective.

1965

Mississippi Band of Choctaw Indians—The Choctaw Housing Authority is organized to provide new houses, renovate older houses, and replace houses lost for Choctaw families on the reservation.

James D. Hale becomes superintendent of the Choctaw Agency in Philadelphia.

1966

Mississippi Band of Choctaw Indians—Phillip Martin is elected president of the Choctaw Community Action Agency.

1969

Mississippi Band of Choctaw Indians—Chahta Development Company is organized on the Pearl River Reservation to provide training and employment to members of the Choctaw tribe and to contract with governmental entities and private organizations in the area, to carry out construction projects.

1970

Congress repeals the Termination Act.

1971

Choctaw Nation of Oklahoma—Harry Belvin becomes the first elected chief of the Choctaw Nation of Oklahoma.

1972

Mississippi Band of Choctaw Indians—The Bureau of Indian Affairs appoints a full-blooded enrolled member of the Choctaw tribe, Robert Benn, as superintendent of the Choctaw Agency in Philadelphia.

1973

The Dancing Rabbit Creek Treaty Site, located in Noxubee County, Mississippi, is declared a national historic landmark.

1974

Jena Band of Choctaw Indians—The "Jena Band of Choctaw Indians of Louisiana" files articles of incorporation. The State of Louisiana legislature passes a resolution formally recognizing "the Choctaw Indian community at Jena, Louisiana, as an Indian tribe" (Gregory, 1977, p. 14).

Jena Band of Choctaw Indians—First elected council of the Jena Band of Choctaw Indians of Louisiana occurs, with Jerry Don Jackson appointed tribal chairperson.

1975

The Indian Self-Determination and Education Assistance Act is passed by Congress.

Choctaw Nation of Oklahoma—David Gardner defeats Belvin in the CNO's second election.

Mississippi Band of Choctaw Indians—Calvin Isaac is elected chief of the Mississippi Band of Choctaw Indians.

Jena Band of Choctaw Indians—Clyde Jackson is elected chairman in the first membership-wide election.

1977
Jena Band of Choctaw Indians—Jena Band completes its tribal center.

1978
Choctaw Nation of Oklahoma—Hollis Roberts becomes chief following Gardner's death.

1979
Mississippi Band of Choctaw Indians—Chahta Enterprise is established as a supplier for Packard Electric to assemble automotive wire harnesses for General Motors. Phillip Martin is reelected chief of the Mississippi Band of Choctaw Indians.

Jena Band of Choctaw Indians—The Jena begin application for federal recognition through the Bureau of Indian Affairs.

1981
Choctaw Nation of Oklahoma—Hollis Roberts is elected chief of the Choctaw Nation of Oklahoma.

1983
Choctaw Nation of Oklahoma—The Choctaw Nation of Oklahoma passes a new constitution.

Mississippi Band of Choctaw Indians—Phillip Martin is reelected.

1984
Jena Band of Choctaw Indians—The Jena Band receives an Administration for Native Americans grant to pursue federal recognition.

1985
Choctaw Nation of Oklahoma—Hollis Roberts is elected to a second term as chief of the Choctaw Nation of Oklahoma.

Jena Band of Choctaw Indians—George Allen is elected tribal chair.

1986
Jena Band of Choctaw Indians—Jerry Don Jackson is elected chairman.

1987
Mississippi Band of Choctaw Indians—Phillip Martin is elected to a third consecutive four-year term as chief.

1988
Congress enacts the Indian Gaming Regulatory Act (IGRA).

Choctaw Nation of Oklahoma—High-stakes bingo operations begin in Durant, Oklahoma.

Jena Band of Choctaw Indians—The Jena Band receives an Administration for Native Americans grant to pursue federal recognition.

1989
Choctaw Nation of Oklahoma—Hollis Roberts is elected to a third term as chief of the Choctaw Nation of Oklahoma.

1990
Jena Band of Choctaw Indians—Jerry Don Jackson is elected to a second term as chair.

1991
Mississippi Band of Choctaw Indians—Phillip Martin is elected to a fourth term as chief of the Mississippi Band of Choctaw Indians.

1993
Choctaw Nation of Oklahoma—Hollis Roberts is elected to his fourth term as chief of the Choctaw Nation of Oklahoma.

1994
Jena Band of Choctaw Indians—Jerry Don Jackson is elected to a third term as chair.

1995
Mississippi Band of Choctaw Indians—Phillip Martin wins a fifth consecutive term as chief of the Mississippi Band of Choctaw Indians.

Jena Band of Choctaw Indians—The Jena Band of Choctaw Indians receives federal recognition as an Indian tribe from the Bureau of Indian Affairs Office of Federal Acknowledgment.

1997
Choctaw Nation of Oklahoma—Hollis Roberts is elected to a fifth term as chief of the Choctaw Nation of Oklahoma.

Choctaw Nation of Oklahoma—Gregory Pyle takes over as chief when Hollis Roberts is found guilty of sexually abusing female tribal employees.

1998
Jena Band of Choctaw Indians—B. Cheryl Smith is elected chief.

1999
Mississippi Band of Choctaw Indians—June 8: Chief Phillip Martin is elected to a sixth consecutive term.

July: The Choctaw Indian Fair celebrates its Fiftieth Anniversary.

2001
Choctaw Nation of Oklahoma—Greg Pyle is elected as chief of the Choctaw Nation of Oklahoma.

2002
Jena Band of Choctaw Indians—Christine Norris is elected chief.

2004
Oklahoma State Tribal Gaming Act passes, which allows the Choctaw to enact casino-style gaming.

2005
Choctaw Nation of Oklahoma—Greg Pyle is elected to a second term as chief of the Choctaw Nation of Oklahoma.

2006
Jena Band of Choctaw Indians—Christine Norris is elected to a second term as chief.

2007
Mississippi Band of Choctaw Indians—Beasley Denson takes the oath of office to become the third chief of the Tribe since adoption of their modern constitution.

2009
Choctaw Nation of Oklahoma—Greg Pyle is elected to a third term as chief of the Choctaw Nation of Oklahoma.

2010
Jena Band of Choctaw Indians—B. Cheryl Smith is elected chief.

2011
Mississippi Band of Choctaw Indians—Phyliss Anderson is sworn in as the first female chief of the Mississippi Band of Choctaw Indians.

2013
Choctaw Nation of Oklahoma—Greg Pyle is elected to a fourth term as chief of the Choctaw Nation of Oklahoma.

Jena Band of Choctaw Indians—The Choctaw Pines Casino opens in Dry Prong, Louisiana.

2014
Choctaw Nation of Oklahoma—Mike Batton becomes chief upon the resignation of Chief Pyle.

Jena Band of Choctaw Indians—B. Cheryl Smith is elected to a second term as chief.

2017
Choctaw Nation of Oklahoma—Mike Batton is elected to his second term as chief of the Choctaw Nation of Oklahoma.

1

The Deep History of the Choctaw

This chapter provides the broad outlines of the shared history for the group of people who became known as the Choctaw. The Choctaw as a group enters the written record shortly after 1540, when the Spanish party accompanying explorer Fernando de Soto encountered them. But their unwritten history extends perhaps as far back as 10,000 years, with the first inhabitants of the southeastern North American continent. Although we do not know what the first groups of people on this continent called themselves, the archaeological record indicates a development of people from early times, through the archaeological record, up to the time of European contact.

Much of the following archaeological summary information is derived from or based on the research of Ian Thompson (2008) and his resultant dissertation titled "*Chahta Intikba Im Aiikhvna* (Learning from the Choctaw Ancestors): Integrating Indigenous and Experimental Approaches in the Study of Mississippian Technologies." Thompson, of Choctaw, Muscogee (Creek), and Euro-American heritage, has served as the Tribal Historic Preservation Officer of the Choctaw Nation of Oklahoma since 2012.

EARLY EXPLORERS OF THE NORTH AMERICAN CONTINENT

Archaeologists are still uncertain about where the first explorers of the North American continent came from. The long-held belief that the first peoples crossed the frozen expanse of the so-called Bering Land Bridge is what most people may have heard. However, that story is no longer accepted as the only (or even most likely) way of arrival of the earliest people.

According to the most commonly known story (e.g., Haynes, 1966), the first people to arrive in the Americas were a group of highly specialized big game hunters who originated somewhere in northeastern Asia. It is proposed that these hunters, following Siberian mammoth herds and other game, crossed the Bering Strait Land Bridge into Alaska sometime around 15,000 years ago, when sea level was lower than it is today because of the amount of seawater that was then tied up in the glaciers. Some archaeologists even suggest that the ancestors of the earliest people to cross into the Western Hemisphere might have lived on the Bering Land Bridge just before the ice began retreating (Hoffecker, Elias, & O'Rourke, 2014). An alternative proposal—that the earliest inhabitants of North America followed the Pacific coast—has gained supporters. With the discovery of early occupations at Monte Verde in Chile during a time when the ice-free corridor would have been impenetrable (Dillehay, 1989), others have proposed the coastal route as a more hospitable route (see Braje et al., 2017; Dillehay, 1997; Dillehay et al., 2015; Dixon, 1999; Erlandson, 2001; Meltzer, 2010).

Regardless of how these early people got into what is now North America, archaeologists believe that these people—or their immediate descendants—developed into what has been called the Clovis archaeological culture, identified by diagnostic projectile points (spear points) with a distinctive flake scar (called a "flute") on their bases. This culture has been dated to between 11,500 and 10,900 BCE (Fiedel, 2000). Clovis groups were highly mobile, and most of what is known about them is derived from campsites associated with large-animal resources. Regardless of their point of entry, the group apparently spread quickly across the deglaciated North and South America. The artifacts they made are found from the Atlantic to the Pacific Coasts, and from Canada to Central America (Collins, 1999; Meltzer, 2010). According to this theory, the highly successful Clovis people represent the direct ancestors of contemporary Native Americans on both continents.

More recently, however, this theory has been questioned for several reasons. It has not been scientifically ascertained exactly when the ice-free corridor opened. The possibility exists that it remained closed until the end of the Clovis period (Wilson & Burnes, 1999). This brings up questions about the timing and possible route of arrival. Mammoth hunting does not seem to have been important in eastern Beringia during the Pleistocene (Dixon, 1999), and Alaska decidedly lacks well-documented early fluted point sites (Clark, 1991). Moreover, the evidence for "pre-Clovis" occupations at several archaeological sites, including Monte Verde in Chile (ca. 12,800 BCE), Meadowcroft in Pennsylvania (ca. 17,300 BCE), and Cactus Hill in Virginia (ca. 16,400 BCE), has been sufficiently convincing for many researchers to accept a "pre-Clovis" human presence in the Americas (e.g., Meltzer et al., 1997).

Based on currently available evidence, the dates now accepted by professional archaeologists for the initial colonization of the Americas range between 12,000 and 20,000 BCE (Dixon, 1999). A similar lack of consensus exists concerning the Asian archaeological cultures and sites that are thought to have been the forerunners of Clovis culture (Fiedel, 2000). Additionally, no particular American archaeological culture has been unanimously identified by archaeologists as a Clovis forebear (Hoffecker, Powers, & Goebel, 1993), although arguments exist for the Denali (West, 1996), the predecessors of Nennana (Goebel, Powers, & Bilge, 1991), Nennana itself (Hoeffecker et al., 1993), and a generalized lanceolate-producing group from the western Americas (Stanford, 1991). In light of these difficulties and apparent contradictions, hypotheses have been forwarded in which initial peopling of the Americas proceeded by boat from Asia (Dixon, 1999) or from Western Europe (Bradley & Stanford, 2004). Recent genetic studies and evidence from archaeological sites indicates that people were spreading throughout the Americas between 14,000 and 15,000 years ago, well before the Clovis period (Anderson & Sassaman, 2004; Goodyear, 2005; Halligan et al., 2016). The majority of the archaeological community continues to accept the idea that the original inhabitants of the Americas arrived from northern Asia (Meltzer, 2002), and many agree that if Clovis was not the first occupation, it was at least the first really important one.

Clovis people lived during the Terminal Pleistocene, in the archaeological cultural period known as Paleoindian, which began with the first evidence of humans on this continent and extended until about 9500 BCE. During this time, high climatic equability allowed the development of plant and animal communities that were unlike any modern analogues (Morse, Anderson, & Goodyear, 1996). From sites such as Blackwater Draw in New Mexico, it is apparent that Clovis people hunted Pleistocene megafauna; sites such as Gault in Texas show that they subsisted on small animals and plants as well.

The most diagnostic implements recovered from a large number of Clovis sites include elaborate bifacial, fluted, stone points and bifaces that served a number of tool functions. More common are cutting and scraping tools made on flakes and blades. General characteristics of Clovis lithic tools include high-quality, often nonlocal, raw material and a high incidence of single implements being used for multiple functions. Less common artifacts

in the Clovis inventory include blades and blade cores; bone and ivory artifacts; small, limited-use features such as hearths; and, very rarely, plant
and small-animal remains (Haynes, 2002). Given its continent-wide spread,
the standardization of Clovis artifacts is truly impressive and suggests a high
level of group mobility. Most researchers would probably agree that Clovis
society was organized in the form of small, flexible, egalitarian groups.

After the continent-wide Clovis manifestation, Paleoindian communities began to diverge. In the Southeast during the two millennia following
Clovis, a number of archaeological cultures now identified by their projectile points came to prominence, including Cumberland, Simpson, Suwanee,
Quad, Beaver Lake, and Dalton. Although variation existed in time and
space, most archaeologists interpret these Paleoindian groups to have had
a number of basic similarities with the characteristics of Clovis described
above. During the terminal Pleistocene, most of the megafauna became
extinct, perhaps because of climate change (Beck, 1996), disease (MacPhee
& Marx, 1997), being overhunted (Martin & Klein, 1984), or a combination of any or all of these reasons.

Pertinent to this is a Choctaw oral tradition explaining the formation
of the Black Belt Prairie along the Tombigbee River, which describes huge
animals that lived in the region at the time when the Choctaw first arrived
in the area:

> These mighty animals broke off the low limbs of the trees in eating
> the leaves, and also gnawed the bark off of the trees, which, in the
> course of time, caused them to wither and die; they roamed in differ-
> ent bands, that engaged in desperate battles whenever and wherever
> they met, and thus caused them to rapidly decrease in numbers; and
> that in the course of years all had perished but two large males, who,
> separate and alone, wandered about for several years—each confin-
> ing himself to the solitude of the forest many miles from the other.
> Finally, in their wanderings they met, and at once engaged in terrible
> conflict in which one was killed. The survivor, now monarch of the
> forests, strolled about for a few years wrapt in the solitude of his own
> reflections and independence—then died, and with him the race
> became extinct. (Cushman, 1899, p. 207)

Despite the appearance of regional traditions at the end of the Paleoindian period, the archaeological connection between the groups that lived
at this time and the Choctaw people is far from specific. Most archaeologists likely see the Choctaw as being descended from Paleoindian forebears
on a general level, but would not venture to make higher resolution

archaeological connections, such as those which might isolate a specific geographic region for Choctaw Pleistocene ancestry, due to a lack of archaeological evidence.

THE ARCHAIC PERIOD

By convention, a new archaeological age, known as the Archaic Period (9500–1250 BCE) commences with the onset of the Holocene climatic event. During this period, more localized cultural traditions became recognizable, with a more diverse array of material objects known from archaeological sites, including baskets, bags, nets, cloth garments, earth ovens, wooden tools, boats, bone pins, needles, awls, and more diverse artwork (e.g., Chapman, 1999; Doran, 1992; Purdy, 1992). In addition, widespread technological innovations include ground stone tools and ornaments, ceramics, and notched stone projectile points (Bense, 1994).

In the Southeast, the Archaic period is divided into three somewhat arbitrary chronological stages: Early (9500–6950 BCE), Middle (6950–3750 BCE), and Late (3750–1250 BCE) (Anderson & Sassaman, 2004; Sassaman & Anderson, 2004). At the beginning of the Early Archaic, hardwood deciduous forests dominated much of the Southeast, as they had during the preceding Paleoindian period (Webb et al., 1993). Early Archaic human communities appear to have concentrated within particular drainages for much of the year and practiced a high degree of residential mobility within relatively small geographic ranges (Anderson & Hanson, 1988). Subsistence was focused on hunting modern animal forms and plant food gathering, particularly mast (nut) crops (Morse et al., 1996).

The Middle Archaic (6950–3750 BCE) period roughly corresponds with the very warm, Hypsithermal climatic event. During this period, modern pine forest spread through much of the Southeast (Webb et al., 1993). Sea level reached its present height, and streams became less rapid and erosive (Schuldenrein, 1996). More permanent settlements developed around expanded riverine resources, notably shellfish (Anderson & Sassaman, 2004). Human-made earth-mounds first appeared in the Southeast during the Middle Archaic, appearing as early as 5200 BCE in northern Louisiana (Gibson & Shenkel, 1989). Many early mounds seem to have been associated with crematory features and often served as repositories for burials. The use of earth mounds and other ceremonial structures spread during the period, along with trading networks (Smith, 1986). New technologies of the Middle Archaic period include grooved axes and atlatl weights. It was also during this time that the earliest incipient agricultural activities conducted in the present-day United States appeared. Crops included sunflower (Crites, 1993), cucurbits and sumpweed (Gremillion, 1996), and chenopod (Smith & Cowan, 1987). No signs of social hierarchy are known from the mid-Archaic Southeast (Fagan, 2000).

The Late Archaic (3750–1250 BCE) begins after the Hypsithermal and coincides with the onset of roughly modern climatic conditions. The adoption of fiber-tempered pottery on the Atlantic Coast of Georgia and South Carolina is the main technological hallmark of the Late Archaic in the Southeast. The use of shellfish intensified in the Late Archaic, and settlements became more substantial, although most were still likely abandoned during the cool season (Anderson & Sassaman, 2004). Lithic trends shifted back somewhat, emphasizing higher-quality nonlocal stone, and curated lithic materials, partially as a result of still-expanding trade (Amick & Carr, 1996). It is unclear whether status differentiation existed within communities in the Late Archaic Southeast.

Considering the Archaic period as a whole, persistent trends include population growth (the number of sites doubled from early to late Archaic [Anderson & Sassaman, 2004]), the localization of subsistence activities, a development of exchange networks, and more permanent settlements. Inhabitants were generally using more local materials and relied heavily on local plant and animal resources, including shellfish and nut crops. Pottery use began in the Southeast and signaled a new technology that would increase dramatically in the following years.

THE WOODLAND PERIOD

Following the Archaic in archaeological terminology is the Woodland period, (700 BCE–1000 CE). The designation of the Woodland period is based more on cultural than environmental developments, and so its dates vary throughout the Southeastern region. The Woodland Period represents an intensification of many of the cultural trends that began during the Archaic, and except for the widespread adoption of the bow late in this period, few entirely new innovations occurred. This local intensification allows archaeologists to use mortuary and ceramic evidence to connect local archaeological cultures with the ethnohistorical Choctaw, in including Marksville and subsequent Baytown and Coles Creek phases from the lower Mississippi valley, the ancestors of the Pensacola phase of the Mobile delta, and communities on the Black Warrior and middle Tombigbee Rivers in west-central Alabama (Galloway, 1995).

Although a great deal of archaeological data contributes to the deep history of the Choctaw, information on developments within the Black

Warrior and middle Tombigbee River valleys of central and western Alabama serves as a general guideline for the cultural period. The Woodland in the Tombigbee region is divided into several stages, including Alexander (850–200 BCE), Miller I (100 BCE–300 CE), Miller II (300–650 CE), and Miller III (650–1000 CE); little information exists for the Black Warrior drainage until the end of the Late Woodland, denoted the West Jefferson (850–1050 CE) archaeological culture by archaeologists.

In the middle Tombigbee valley, the local variant of Alexander can be viewed as a transition period between Late Archaic and Early Woodland. Material culture includes fiber-tempered pottery and projectile points, which suggest continuity with earlier archaeological cultures in the area (Ensor, 1980). During the spring and summer, the valley's residents lived in large camps on the edges of meadows, where deer hunting would have been productive. In late summer, aquatic resources were sought in the lowlands. During the cool months, residential units separated, with small groups moving into the woods to take advantage of mast crops and the mammals they attracted (Jenkins & Krause, 1986). The latter part of this stage is recognized by the replacement of fiber as the primary pottery temper with sand. Population increases required more focused subsistence reliance on deer hunting and mast crop gathering, and smaller mammals, birds, and aquatic resources were also important (Jenkins & Krause, 1986).

Locally, Miller I (100 BCE–300 CE) corresponds with the broader Middle Woodland period developments. This time period also represents the height of Hopewellian influence in the Southeast (Hally & Mainfort, 2004). Various "exotic" artifacts and artifact types occur in the area in this time period, including cord- and fabric-marked pottery; new house types; burial mounds; and more exotic goods, including silver panpipes, galena, copper, greenstone celts, and trade pots and projectile points. This influx of materials has led archaeologists to hypothesize that Miller I represents an intrusion into the area by a group indigenous to Tennessee (Jenkins & Krause, 1986). Despite these developments toward "complexity," the use of exotic stone for utilitarian tools decreased, while heat treating of local river cobbles became commonplace (Ensor, 1980).

Residents lived in moderately sized settlements located in the floodplain forest, with many of them situated near earth mounds. Food resources included mostly aquatic and local forest resources, with abundant shell middens developing as a result. During the winter, people moved to smaller settlements scattered through the region, to hunt and collect in a diversity of environments (Jenkins & Krause, 1986). Based on inference concerning the organization needed to construct the earth mounds, as well as the differential burial treatment given to individuals within them, it has been hypothesized that Miller I represents the beginnings of a hierarchical society within the valley.

In the middle Tombigbee, Miller II appears to have developed in place from Miller I, with the new phase recognized based on an increasing emphasis on cord-marked, grog-tempered pottery (Peebles & Mann, 1983). Thermal alteration of siliceous stone also increased, with heat-treated stone comprising 95 percent of Miller II debitage (Ensor, 1980). Significant population growth is evident between Miller I and Miller II (Brown, 2004). As a result of the population growth, subsistence focus shifted away from deer slightly, with increasing emphasis on "second-line" resources such as small mammals, fish, mast crops, and starchy seeds such as chenopodium (Jenkins & Ensor, 1982), perhaps as a result of resource stress (Jenkins, 1982).

Miller III (also known as the Baytown phase) appears to have developed in place from Miller II (Jenkins & Krause, 1986). This phase is signaled by the appearance of small, triangular arrow points (Ensor, 1981), with heat treating performed at a higher temperature than previously, along with the decreasing of the size of most tools and debitage (Ensor, 1980). The abundance of ground stone artifacts also decreased during the period. Grog tempering of pottery gained in popularity over sand tempering, but a small amount of shell-tempered pottery showed up near the end of the period. Although nonlocal items became more common at the end of Miller III, and external influence is evident (Galloway, 1995), there is no local evidence for status differentiation.

Corn made its first appearance in the middle Tombigbee region during Miller III but remained rare through the period. In addition to the adoption of corn during this period, the use of mast crops increased significantly (Caddell, 1981). Seeds from a large number of indigenous annuals also became more common in the region, although their frequency still does not suggest a particularly strong horticultural focus (Blitz, 1993). Deer remains in archaeological deposits continued to decrease from Miller I levels, while those of smaller mammals, birds, snakes, reptiles, and aquatic resources increased (Jenkins & Krause, 1986).

Miller III seems to have maintained the residence pattern of Miller II, but there was an increase in the number of settlements. Lowland occupation, particularly near mussel beds, became more substantial (Blitz, 1983). Rectangular-shaped houses replaced the oval house shape of previous periods. Although population increase is evident, the geographic range of Miller III contracted from that of Miller II (Jenkins & Krause, 1986). At the same time, evidence for interpersonal violence appears (Hill, 1981).

THE MISSISSIPPIAN PERIOD

In much of the Southeast, the Woodland period was followed by the Mississippian period. The Mississippian is marked by human populations existing in the eastern deciduous woodlands during the time period 800–1500 CE. A ranked form of social organization existed in the populations, along with a specific complex adaptation to linear, environmentally circumscribed floodplain habitat zones (Smith, 1978). Common Mississippian material traits include permanent residence (with little or no seasonal migrations), hunting and warfare with the bow and arrow, shell-tempered pottery, pyramidal earth mounds, a regionalized similarity in ideology (Southeastern Ceremonial Complex), and a number of visible artistic forms with certain recurrent motifs. As defined by archaeology, the Mississippian phenomenon showed up in different times in different places, with some Southeastern communities never participating.

Modern Choctaw Mississippian ancestry apparently lies in the Mississippian cultures of the Plaquemine phases of the lower Mississippi valley, the Bottle Creek phases of the Mobile delta, the Lyons Bluff and Sorrels phases in central Mississippi, the Moundville phases of the Black Warrior River in west-central Alabama, and the Summerville phases of the middle Tombigbee River (Carleton, 1994; Galloway, 1995). As a mechanism toward simplification, the chapter focuses primarily on developments in two areas—the Moundville site in the Black Warrior valley and the Lubbub Creek site in the middle Tombigbee drainage.

Moundville

The Moundville site in central Alabama is the second largest precolonial construction north of Mexico, contiguously occupying 75 hectares (about 185 acres). It includes at least 29 earth mounds as well as a bastioned palisade that was rebuilt several times over the course of the site's occupation (Knight & Steponaitis, 1998). Moundville's chronology is divided into Moundville I (1050–1250 CE), Moundville II (1250–1400 CE), Moundville III (1400–1550 CE), and Moundville IV (1550–1650 CE) periods, with Moundville IV also known as the Burial Urn Culture or the Alabama River phase.

Construction began around 1050 CE, featuring the Mississippian hallmarks of platform mounds and square dwellings with wall-trench architecture. Moundville rapidly became a dense settlement, while the remainder of the valley's inhabitants also appears to have given up small nuclear settlement in favor of dispersed farmsteads (Knight & Steponaitis, 1998).

Aerial view of Mound B at the Mississippian site of Moundville (1000 to 1450 CE) in present-day Alabama. Mississippian archaeological cultures were the forerunners of contemporary Southeastern Indian tribes. (iStockphoto.com)

At the beginning of Moundville I, subsistence on nuts declined precipitously from levels during previous times, but the resources retained some importance. Cultivation of indigenous plants continued—beans were introduced, and corn came to provide up to 40 percent of caloric intake (Scarry, 1998). Deer hunting was important, but fish contributed 25 percent of the protein to local diets (Schoeninger & Schurr, 1998).

The only mounds known to have been erected in the Black Warrior Valley during early Moundville I were located at the Moundville site. Previous centers in the vicinity were abandoned, but new ones were constructed (Knight & Steponaitis, 1998). Archaeologists view these developments as evidence of social differentiation, and the existence of Moundville as a regional center even at its inception (Welch, 1998). At around 1250 CE, at the end of Moundville I, the Moundville polity had become a highly structured, complex chiefdom with three levels of decision-making (Welch & Scarry, 1995), directly controlling a 30- to 50-kilometer stretch of the Black Warrior Valley (Welch, 1991) and incorporating perhaps 10,000 people (Knight & Steponaitis, 1998).

All mounds known from the site were under construction in late Moundville I. Arranged symmetrically around a plaza, they may have been a sociogram, representing ranked clan order (Knight, 1998). At the same time, residents moved inside of a palisade constructed around the site (Steponaitis, 1998). During Moundville I, the abundance of nonlocal goods reached the highest frequency that they would ever attain at the site (Blitz, 1993). At the same time, specialization in lithic manufacture, shell bead manufacture, and pottery production began in certain precincts (Ensor, 1981). By the end of Moundville I, maize was providing 65 percent of the caloric intake, and it appears that commoners from the outlying communities were supplying Moundville's elite with processed food (Welch & Scarry, 1995).

Interpretation of the following Moundville II period is a period of entrenchment by the elite. Their burials were clearly distinguished by levels of grave goods, including shell beads, copper gorgets, copper ear spools, copper-bladed axes, monolithic axes, stone paint pallets, and galena, as well as the apparent sacrifice of retainers (Knight & Steponaitis, 1998). However, by the end of Moundville II at 1300 CD, most of Moundville's inhabitants vacated it, with the site serving more as a necropolis for the polity's population, inhabited mostly by the elite and their retainers (Steponaitis, 1998), rather than a generalized population.

The site continued to lose population during Moundville III and IV, resulting in its ultimate abandonment. Proposed dates and reasons for abandonment vary from the 1400s (Peebles, 1986) to the 1500s (Brain & Phillips, 1996). At about this same time, southeastern society appears to have reverted to a less socially structured one, with Southeastern Ceremonial Complex items associated with more classes of people; nucleated settlements founded at different regions in the valley for the first time since Moundville I; and outlying communities of the period becoming increasingly self-sufficient (Knight & Steponaitis, 1998). During Moundville IV, subsistence in the region shifted back in favor of wild foods (Schoeninger & Schurr, 1998); social organization shrunk to the village level; and the trappings of Mississippian nobility entirely disappeared (Welch, 1998). A few mounds were occupied at Moundville until about 1600, when the site was completely vacated. By 1650, the majority of the Black Warrior River Valley's once very large population had apparently moved to other regions (Knight & Steponaitis, 1998).

Lubbub Creek

Because of Moundville's size and influence, the occurrences just described impacted to some degree contemporaneous events in the nearby middle Tombigbee region (Brown, 2004; Peebles, 1983b). As a partial result of this, the local Mississippian period is divided into Summerville

I (1050–1200 CE), Summerville II–III (1200–1500 CE), and Summerville IV (ca 1500–1600 CE) phases, which are temporally equivalent with the Moundville I–IV phases just discussed (Blitz, 1993). Yet despite the connections and some similarities, Mississippian communities living in the middle Tombigbee clearly followed their own course, differing from Moundville communities in several fundamental ways (e.g., Peebles, 1987).

Within the middle Tombigbee valley, the Lubbub Creek site, in Pickens County, Alabama, has been both well studied and partially destroyed as a result of the Tennessee-Tombigbee Waterway Project (Blitz, 1993; Peebles, 1983a). Ian Thompson, in his dissertation research (2008), identified Lubbub Creek as an ancestral Choctaw settlement because of its location, particular subsistence pattern, burial practice, and ceramics tradition that held sway late in its occupation, and their equivalents among early colonial Choctaw communities, but which are different from those of other local tribes. To date, the Lubbub Creek site is one of the best-studied, ancestral Choctaw settlements from the time period.

The Lubbub Creek settlement was located within a sharp, interior bend of the Tombigbee River, where it intersected with a smaller stream called Lubbub Creek in close proximity to patches of Black Belt Prairie and forest, slope and terrace forests, and river and creek floodplains. Together, these diverse ecosystems offered a great deal of plant and animal diversity as well as a variety of mineral resources (cf. Ensor, 1981), including good soils for agriculture (Cole, 1983). The site had a long human history, having been intermittently inhabited since the Early Archaic period. At the end of Miller III, it served as a base camp that was uninhabited during the winter (Blitz, 1993; Peebles, 1983c). During the Mississippian, it became a permanently inhabited village, surrounded by small hamlets whose inhabitants appear to have spent time at Lubbub Creek, particularly during the cool months (Blitz, 1993).

During the Summerville I period, the Lubbub Creek settlement was 8.5 hectares (21 acres) in extent (Peebles, 1983c). A sharp-angled pyramid mound with two ramps was at the settlement's center, with a large plaza to the east (Blitz, 1983). A series of clay-covered walls made of upright logs, standing about 2 meters high, surrounded the plaza and mound on at least their south and west sides, and cut off land access to the settlement from the west. The north, east, and south sides were bordered by the Tombigbee River (Cole & Albright, 1983). A doughnut-shaped residential area, believed to have served both as a permanent dwelling place for a few elite, and as a winter home for at least a portion of the dispersed farming community, existed outside of the last of these walls (Blitz, 1993). Some archaeologists believe that perhaps only one to six houses were occupied at a given time (Peebles, 1983c).

Southeastern Ceremonial Complex materials and pottery essentially identical to that found at Moundville suggest that Summerville I people at Lubbub Creek maintained close contacts with the polity to the east (Welch, 1998), even though there is no evidence of direct Moundville control (Peebles, 1983b). Common elements of Lubbub Creek's material culture are essentially identical with those found on contemporary sites on the upper Tombigbee in Mississippi (Blitz, 1993), indicating contacts in this direction as well. A microlith and shell bead manufacturing industry at Lubbub Creek hints that some individuals may have been involved in a form of labor specialization (Ensor, 1981). There is evidence for both some status differentiation and warfare. It's possible that during Summerville I and through most of the Mississippian, Lubbub Creek may have been the center of a simple chiefdom allied with, but not subordinate to, Moundville.

During this time, the Lubbub Creek subsistence pattern became more heavily focused on maize (Caddell, 1983), with the consumption of wild and domestic plant foods balanced with a greater concentration on mammals, particularly deer, than had been the case during Miller III (Scott, 1983). Subsistence stayed basically the same through Summerville III, with small game taken during the warm months at the homesteads around the Lubbub Creek site, and focused hunts for larger game conducted communally during the cool season (Blitz, 1993; Hudson, 1997; Scott, 1983).

The Summerville II and III (1200–1450 CE) are identified by the appearance of the Moundville Engraved ceramic variety and have been interpreted to represent particularly close interaction between the Tombigbee centers and Moundville (Blitz, 1993). During this time, there is a peak in the abundance of nonlocal artifacts, which were distributed in a more egalitarian fashion than at Moundville (Blitz, 1993; Welch & Scarry, 1995), as well as a slight increase in the subsistence focus on maize (Caddell, 1983). The Summerville II–III Lubbub Creek community grew slightly larger, with an estimated 5 to 18 houses being occupied at any given time (Peebles, 1983c). At the beginning of the period, or soon into it, the palisades were done away with, and several more construction levels were added onto the mound (Blitz, 1983).

Summerville IV (1450–ca. 1600 CE) is identified by the discontinuation of Moundville Engraved pottery and the concomitant appearance of Alabama River ceramics. During this time, a defensive ditch was dug on at the western side, and perhaps all the way around the Lubbub Creek settlement, which had decreased in size. At one time, a wooden palisade probably bordered the inner side of the trench (Albright, 1983). Only an estimated two to seven houses were simultaneously occupied within it (Peebles, 1983c). During Summerville IV, reliance on maize decreased significantly in favor of acorns (Caddell, 1983), and the abundance of nonlocal trade materials declined sharply (see Blitz, 1993, Figs. 48–51).

Thompson (2008) gives an interesting example relating to this time period that might be preserved in the Choctaw language. He notes that

---

TRIBAL HISTORIC PRESERVATION OFFICES

In 1992, amendments to the National Historic Preservation Act allowed tribes to take over functions of the states to protect historic properties of importance to the tribes on their tribal land. In 1996, 12 tribes were certified by the National Park Service to undertake historic preservation programs on tribal lands; as of May 2018, 179 tribes have been certified to do so.

Tribal Historic Preservation Offices (THPOs) work primarily to ensure that federal agencies comply with the National Historic Preservation Act (NHPA) and other federal laws established for the protection of environmental and cultural resources that may be impacted by federal undertakings. They work closely with state and local agencies through Compliance and Review and government-to-government consultation. THPOs locate and document sites of cultural and spiritual significance to the tribe to ensure their perpetuity and protection, and also serve as repositories for archaeological records and historical documents. In addition, THPOs also serve to help preserve other aspects of culture such as language conservation and revitalization; oral history interviews; and work to repatriate human remains, funerary items, sacred objects, and objects of cultural patrimony held by federal agencies or museums, or that were intentionally excavated or inadvertently discovered on federal or tribal lands through the Native American Graves Protection and Repatriation Act (NAGPRA).

In 2003, the Choctaw Nation of Oklahoma was formally certified as eligible to take over the role of the state historic preservation officer on tribal lands. In May 2018, Dr. Ian Thompson was the Tribal Historic Preservation Officer for the Choctaw Nation of Oklahoma.

In 2010, the Jena Band of Choctaw Indians was officially designated by the National Park Service as qualified to take over the role of the state to protect properties of importance to the Band. In May 2018, Ms. Alina Shively was the Tribal Historic Preservation Officer for the Jena Band of Choctaw Indians.

The Mississippi Band of Choctaw Indians has not applied for certification by the National Park Service to take over the role of the state on tribal lands, but this does not preclude the Mississippi Band's involvement in the historic preservation process. In May 2018, Kenneth Carleton was the Historic Preservation Official for the Mississippi Band of Choctaw Indians.

the word *Tombigbee* is a corruption of the Choctaw phrase *itombi ikbi*, meaning literally "coffin makers," who were said to have lived on its banks (Byington, 1915). The ancestral Choctaw who inhabited this valley during Summerville IV, along with related peoples living on the Alabama River, were formerly known archaeologically as the "Burial Urn Culture" because of their notable practice of using large Alabama River ceramic vessels as elaborate burial urns to house secondary human interments. Although it cannot likely be proven, the Choctaw term for the river could possibly be a linguistic memorial of the practice that was conducted there.

INTO THE COLONIAL ERA

Europeans entered the Southeast during the Summerville IV time span. Although at present the archaeological chronology is too inexact to determine for certain, it is possible that many of the Summerville IV changes outlined above were the result of some of the turmoil of the first waves of European diseases entering the region, perhaps before any Europeans did. As outlined in the following chapter, the De Soto expedition came into western Alabama in October 1540. Recent reconstructions of De Soto's journey place the Lubbub Creek site directly (see Brain, 1985, duplicated in Galloway (1995, Fig. 3.2)) or within a very few kilometers of their path (see Hudson, 1997, Map 7). No Spanish materials were recovered from the site, and there is little mention in the expedition accounts of encountering Native communities in the area, until reaching the Upper Tombigbee, where, on two occasions, they were nearly finished off by a group calling themselves the "Chicasa" (now known as the Chickasaw). The site continued to be inhabited for several generations after De Soto.

Archaeologists believe that the main populations of the middle Tombigbee and Moundville regions moved to the west and south in the 1600s (Blitz, 1993; Galloway, 1995). It is unknown exactly when the last resident left the Lubbub Creek site, but European records indicate that the area was vacated of permanent settlement by 1700 CE (Peebles, 1983c). Peebles attributes the abandonment of the Lubbub Creek site to slaving raids from the Muscogee (Creek) and other groups funded by the English colonies to the east, noting evidence of the palisade burning at the very end of the site's occupation (Peebles, 1983c). The descendants of the people living at Lubbub Creek, along with some of those from Moundville and the Pensacola, Plaquemine, and Pearl River Mississippian groups, are believed by anthropologists to have formed a Choctaw confederation in east-central Mississippi and west-central Alabama before 1700 CE (Carleton, 1994; Galloway, 1995). The Lubbub Creek site was within the borders of these Choctaw lands, and a few pieces of 1800s Choctaw pottery recovered there show that the site was at least occasionally revisited.

The precise manner in which all of the specific ancestral Mississippian groups contributed to the Choctaw Tribe as it existed at the time of European encounters and the European colonial period is not perfectly known, but some of the complexity is preserved in 1700s French colonial documents. The boundaries of the Choctaw Tribe were fluid and difficult for the Europeans to ascertain. The Naniaba, Tohoma, Bayogoula Pascagoula, Acopissa, Houma, Chitamacha, Napochi, Quinipissa, and Tangipahoa Tribes all lived in the vicinity of the Choctaw; shared a variety of cultural similarities, including language; and often formed close political ties with Choctaw "proper" (Pesantubbee, 2005; Swanton, 1946). The Choctaw Tribe is known to have regularly adopted various individuals and villages into their confederation, and is believed in several instances to have incorporated entire tribes, including the Chakchiuma, Chatot, Ibitoupa, Choula, Mobile, Okelousa, Pensacola, and Tohome (Swanton, 1946). Sometimes, the adopted tribes formed their own villages within the Choctaw Tribe that retained their original group names. It is also evident that the various villages comprising the Choctaw Tribe had a high level of political autonomy, as evidenced in the Choctaw Civil War of 1747–1750. This flexibility through adaptation, alliance building, adoption, and amalgamation was a mechanism effectively employed by the Choctaw and their neighbors to survive the extreme population loss and upheaval caused by colonialist encounters with Europeans.

Many Choctaw oral traditions unquestionably deal with the time period outlined in this chapter and connect the Choctaw people to the homeland. Through this, they provide a human meaning to the past. As Thompson (2008) notes, "The primary importance of the archaeological story becomes not so much the cold specifics of changes in material culture through time, or even measures of human social organization, but rather that all of these things are a part of the history, of a living, persisting, vibrant human group: the Choctaw people" (p. 108).

2

❖

Interactions with European Cultures

Numerous European authors wrote about the people they encountered whom they called the Choctaw. Most of the information about the Choctaw prior to the American period of interaction is derived from early accounts of Spaniards who accompanied De Soto; French traders and functionaries who interacted with them; and, of course, later English and Americans. At the time of European contact, the Choctaw were essentially a confederation of allied people who shared a generally common language and a relatively common culture. As in the previous chapter, the natives of the Southeast were suddenly and chaotically impacted by a global economy.

Early sources on the Choctaw include Adair (1775), Bartram (1791), Bossu (1771), Du Pratz (1758), and Romans ([1775] 1999), to name but a few. Most of these sources were used by early writers and ethnographers of the later nineteenth century to create a picture of the Choctaw during the early periods of interaction with the Europeans. Bushnell (1909), Cushman (1899), Halbert (1902), and Swanton (1911, 1918, [1931] 2001), among others, used the earlier narratives as "source materials" for further studies. More contemporary writers who have written about the Choctaw include Debo ([1934] 1961), Galloway (1995), Hudson (1976), Kidwell (2008), and Lambert (2007a, 2007b), again to name a few; and other small books created for the general public include McKee (1989) and Sonneborn (2007). The following section, meant to set the stage for Choctaw culture prior to the time of intensive European interaction, relies heavily on Galloway and Kidwell's (2004) encyclopedic entry on the Choctaw in the *Handbook of North American Indians.*

ETHNOGRAPHIC INFORMATION ON THE CHOCTAW

Galloway and Kidwell (2004) recognize that the impact of Europeans on the Choctaw culture in the late eighteenth century creates a difficulty in reconstructing the culture that existed prior to contact. However, based on the early sources, they provide what can be considered to be an accurate portrayal of the social structures that were in place at the time of contact, the geographical situations of the "tribe," and the generalized culture that separated the Choctaw from other groups in the area.

At the time of contact, most of the division of labor was based on gender. Men ranged far and wide as they hunted to provide meat, while women, children, and elders generally stayed nearer to the settlements and fields. Villages were generally comprised of homesteads occupied by family groups of various-sized segments of a lineage. Once the deerskin trade began in earnest, however, things changed: men were more strongly involved in procuring deer skins as trade items (rather than as materials for personal use) and had less time to assist in farming, and the women were required to spend more time in hide preparation. Ultimately, it is possible that this shift in profit derived from "men's work," as opposed to the more heavy reliance on products of "women's labor," might have led to a shift away from cultivation as the basic subsistence mode (Galloway & Kidwell, 2004).

Swanton ([1931] 2001) notes that the Choctaw were the most accomplished farmers in the Southeast in the late eighteenth century. Both men and women participated in planting and harvesting crops of corn, beans, squash, pumpkins, melons, and sunflowers. Men used the time between planting and harvesting to hunt or go to war, while children protected the crops from animals. Crops were supplemented by wild plant products gathered nearby, as well as by fish taken from neighboring water sources. Hunts were often communal events until the introduction of European guns replaced bows and arrows as the primary weapon, but blowguns and throwing sticks continued to be used for smaller game by younger boys as a means of contributing to the subsistence strategies.

The Choctaw had summer and winter structures as well as other structures of various uses. Summer houses were large and rectangular, with entry through a single doorway. The gable ends of the houses had openings to allow smoke to escape. Cane platforms about two feet high abutted the walls and served as seats and beds. The winter houses were smaller and circular, with only one door. Elevated granaries used to store corn were created, with wooden posts as walls and with the spaces between the posts filled with plant material and then covered with clay (wattle-and-daub construction). All the structures had thatched roofs. Each of the towns had a central open space, or town square.

Prior to European contact, men wore a breechcloth with moccasins and leggings for traveling or hunting, while women wore skirts reaching to the knees, and moccasins as well. Galloway and Kidwell (2004) note that reliance on manufactured clothing of European design replaced skins and traditional textiles early in the eighteenth century. Personal adornment included necklaces, sashes, collar gorgets, earrings, and bracelets made of shell and other natural materials, but metalwork soon replaced the majority of the natural items in ornaments. More permanent types of adornment included tattooing on the face and body, as well as a form of skull shaping that resulted in a more flattened forehead.

Choctaw social organization was comprised of three social groupings—*moieties*, *iksas*, and local groups. Although a more exact understanding of the relationships implied by these structures is no longer possible, it was thought they corresponded to a web of diplomatic, ethnic, and genealogical relationships of some historical depth (O'Brien, 2002). *Moieties* were groups comprised of various *iksas* that bore relationships among themselves, and were very important in determining marriage availability and other social restrictions. *Iksas* were comprised of kinship groups interpreted by early writes as submoieties, lineages, or maybe "clans." These groups were also separated spatially within the various towns and districts that made up the Choctaw territory in Mississippi and Alabama.

Choctaw kinship was primarily matrilineal—that is, relationships traced through the mother's line—with kinship ties through the father's side relatively unimportant. Spoehr (1947) noted that the relationships between brother and sister, and between maternal relatives, were especially important.

Choctaw males were divided into four ranks. First were the chiefs—grand chiefs, village chiefs, and war chiefs. Next were the "beloved men," or *hatak holitopa*. Third were the *tushka*, or "warriors," and last were the *hatak imatahalo*, "supporting men," comprised of youth, men who had not struck a blow in war, or men who had killed only a woman or a child in battle. These ranks were also crosscut by age categories, with various status limitations determined by age, relationship with "warriors," and other non-battle strictures. Swanton (1918) wrote that nonparticipants could become a warrior by actions of a victorious father or uncle through a coming-of-age ceremony. Unfortunately, there is not a great deal of information available about any such status ranking among females, most likely because of the European predilection to interact with males as the supposed "head of household" rather than considering that the females might have more status.

Marriages and weddings were based on rules that required the husband and wife to be from separate kinship groups. Marriage marked the beginning of a woman's maternal role within the tribe, and more often the new couple lived in the woman's village (Bushnell, 1909). Children who have lost a parent or parents due to divorce or death generally remained with the woman's family. The Choctaw also practiced "mother-in-law avoidance," whereby a husband and the wife's mother were obligated to avoid each other's company.

Death among the Choctaw provided the most ritualistic ceremony. Upon death, the person's body was covered and placed inside a bark coffin, which was then situated on a scaffold. The body was provided food and drink, extra shoes, ornaments, and weapons. The body remained on the scaffold for as long as six months, and this period was considered a public mourning period. Once the mourning period was complete and the body decomposed, a specialized group of people—"bone pickers" or "bone gatherers"—carefully cleaned the bones of remaining flesh using fingernails that were grown long for the specific purpose. The bones were deposited in a mortuary box or cane basket painted red. After a funerary feast (where the French were disgusted to note that the bone pickers used their hands, without first washing them, to distribute the meal to the participants), the mortuary box was carried to a bone house (or charnel house) to join the other dead (Swanton, [1931] 2001). After the bone house became full, the chests were removed to another place for general interment.

Choctaw government prior to European formalization was organized much like their kinships and family structures. Moieties and matrilineages were the basic organizational structures for both political and ceremonial life within each Choctaw town. Each town had a head chief and a spokesman for the head chief (*tishu mingo*) who arranged ceremonies, feasts, and other celebrations. Other positions of leadership were also named. Similar patterns were in existence at the district level and included a leadership structure that united towns and lineages.

Originally, the Choctaws were located throughout east-central Mississippi and west-central Alabama in independent societies. Districts maintained their own chiefs and other leaders well into the nineteenth century. These separate groups first joined together sometime after 1540 (when Hernando De Soto's expedition devastated the Southeast with disease) and before 1699 (upon the French arrival on the Gulf Coast). By the eighteenth century, the Choctaw were divided into three geographic and political divisions that reflected the makeup and diverse ethnic origins of the Choctaw: the western division, dispersed around the upper Pearl River watershed; the eastern division, situated around the upper Chickasawhay River and lower Tombigbee River watersheds; and the southern division (or Six Towns), located along the upper Leaf River and mid-Chickasawhay River watersheds.

Swanton ([1931] 2001) indicates that the three districts were relatively autonomous and operated independently from the others. More often, major decisions were reached at district councils, with the chief or his spokesperson opening the meeting with a speech stating the issue under consideration. The oldest and most distinguished men led the discussion, followed by others (Pesantubbee, 1999). In this manner, consensus of the people present was reached concerning important decisions.

The major ceremony among the Choctaw, and the southeastern tribes in general, was the Green Corn Dance, although there are no detailed early descriptions of the ceremony (Swanton, [1931] 2001). The ceremony marked the beginning of the political cycle, and new laws and kinship relationships

Illustration by George Catlin shows Choctaw men and boys playing a ball game similar to lacrosse, near Fort Gibson, Indian Territory (now Oklahoma), 1840s. Choctaw "stickball" often involved hundreds of participants and could go on for days until a winner was declared. (Library of Congress)

were discussed for the following year. Swanton concluded that the Choctaw were less ceremonially developed than the other southeastern tribes, instead choosing to spend more time on social dances and feasts, including the eagle dance (Catlin, 1844) and the ball game/night dances held in fall and early winter (Galloway & Kidwell, 2004).

The Choctaw adopted Christian religion early on, but initial beliefs were tied to the sun, symbolized by fire. Agriculture had a strong dependence on the sun, which therefore was held in great esteem. Each man carried a charm or fetish to protect himself from evil spirits, and dreams were powerful omens. Dupumeux, in a letter to written to Beauchamp in 1751, noted that just the dream of defeat by a war leader could be enough to cause the war party to return (Dupumeux, 1751).

Although the Choctaw have been presented as both less likely to invade others' territory by choice and fond of war, war was an important means whereby men were able to achieve status within Choctaw society (Bossu, 1771). Decisions to enter into war were made by a council. The leader of the war party did so more through persuasion rather than by command or dint of office. If the war party was unsuccessful, the war leader was reduced in rank to that of a common warrior. Peacemaking rituals are

---

CHOCTAW STICKBALL

Stickball, or *kapucha toli*, as it is in known in the Choctaw language, has been called the granddaddy of all field sports. Its roots go back centuries, as a forerunner of lacrosse, and it is one of the oldest organized games played in America. In this game, each player has sticks, and there are many players on the field, with high-impact collisions being just a part of the game. The rules are straightforward. Each player has two sticks (*kapucha*) with which to pick up and carry the ball (*towa*) and try to get it to touch the goal (*fabvssa*), a post about four inches in diameter and about 12 feet high. A player can shoot or throw the ball at the goal with his sticks, or, if he can get close enough, he can touch the goal with his sticks while holding the ball within them. The field of play is about the size of an American football field or a soccer field, and many games are played on local high school fields.

George Catlin described a Choctaw stickball game in 1834 in which the teams had several hundred players each. Stickball was played from 1830 until about 1930 in southeastern Oklahoma, and then went by the wayside for a time. In Mississippi, the sport has been big for longer. Choctaw, Mississippi, is the host of the World Series of Stickball played annually at the Choctaw Indian Fair, arguably the biggest, most hotly contested Indigenous ballgame in the country.

poorly represented in early writings, but Swanton ([1931] 2001) notes that a large red pipe was smoked to seal the decision. Galloway (1995) also suggests that gifting of white deerskins helped establish a peaceful path.

THE SPANISH INVASION

Spanish conquistadors, led by Hernando De Soto, came into the lands of western Muskogean-speakers in what is now western Alabama in October 1540 (Hudson, 1976). Soon, De Soto came to Atahachi, the town where Tuscaloosa lived, placed him in chains, and demanded burden bearers and women from him. Tuscaloosa directed the Spanish to the town of Mabila, leading them to believe their lusts would there be fulfilled. Along the journey, the Spanish pillaged local settlements (Rangel, 1540, as cited in Clayton, Knight, & Moore, 1993). De Soto's original intent had been to annex the land, take its resources, and enslave its population. Yet after the battle the Spanish conquistadors came to the view that "it was impossible to rule such bellicose people or to subjugate such bold men . . . it seemed . . . that neither by force nor by persuasion could they be brought under the authority and dominion of the Spaniards; they would allow themselves to be killed first" (Garcilaso [1596] 1993, p. 356). After roughly four weeks of healing from wounds, De Soto's army traveled northward, again pillaging and taking another hostage; the Spanish soon left the area, crossing the Mississippi River in 1541 and entering into what is now Arkansas (Elvas, [1557] 1993). De Soto died in 1542, but roughly half of the expedition survived to return to Mexico (Hudson, 1976).

The Spanish continued to maintain territory in what would become the United States in the Southeast (the Floridas) and the west, but interactions with the Choctaw were less frequent after their initial encounters until much later, when the Choctaw fought with the French during the War of Spanish Succession. Following the Treaty of Paris in 1863, whereby France lost most of its empire in North America, the Spanish regained some influence in the area, but interactions between the Spanish and the Choctaw were still infrequent.

RELATIONS WITH THE FRENCH

After the De Soto expedition, the area's inhabitants had more direct contact with Europeans, and those who came into the region noted wide-ranging effects of contact on local communities (see Hudson, 1997). Some anthropologists have inferred that the Choctaw (*Chahta*) tribe itself formed during this time as a result of the upheaval of war and disease, because it is during late 1600s that the specific name *Chahta* first appears in European texts and maps (Galloway, 1995; Woods, 1978).

In 1698, Frenchman Pierre Le Moyne, Sieur d'Iberville, led the initial expedition to establish the colony of Louisiana. Good relations with the Indians meant allies who would help the French hold on to this colony in the face of English or Spanish, threat of conquest. From the beginning, French relations differed with the important tribes of the colony, the Choctaw, the Chickasaw, and the Natchez. French relations with the Choctaw, based as they were on the fur trade and involving no settlement on the Indians' lands, were generally good. By the end of January 1702, D'Iberville had organized a peace mission to the Choctaw and the Chickasaw; seven Choctaw chiefs and three Chickasaw chiefs arrived at the Mobile post on March 25.

The French settlements in "Louisiana" relied on the populous Choctaw tribe as an ally in trading and warfare, while the more northerly Chickasaw were similarly allied with the English colonies to the east (Pesantubbee, 2005). The rival European powers successfully exploited a preexisting animosity along with economic promises, Indigenous concepts of reciprocity, social ties, and often tactics of sabotaging peace efforts, to entice the Choctaw and Chickasaw (former members of the same tribe according to oral tradition) to face each other in a long series of bloody conflicts.

The French were concerned with maintaining the Choctaw as allies for two reasons: the French preferred the Choctaw to trade with them, rather than with the English to the east, and as military partners. By the end of the War of Spanish Succession in 1714, the French and Choctaw were partners in French-settled North America (Woods, 1978). The Choctaw served many of the French needs, but much of the Choctaw "allegiance" was purchased through trade goods.

As Woods (1978) noted in her review of the relations between French North America ("Louisiana") and the American Indian population of the region, French goods decisively affected the lives and culture of the Choctaw people. In addition to clothing, the French provided iron and brass pots, metal knives, axes, and hoes. In addition to these and the usual trinkets such as combs, pipes, and buttons, the French also provided muskets to replace the bows and arrows that had served as weapons for war and hunting for centuries.

The Choctaw served as military allies for the French during North American actions against Spain in 1719, as well as against the Chickasaw throughout much of the period of French influence in the area. As noted earlier, the Chickasaw alliance with the British served more as an economic threat than a military one. Still, by using the Choctaw to attack the Chickasaw, the French hoped to keep English influence from seeping into their trading realm. By 1725, Choctaw loyalty and reliability as partners with the French was unquestioned.

A dichotomy of alliances within the tribe was similarly exploited by the French and the English to precipitate a disastrous Choctaw civil war of 1747–1750, while a simultaneous wave of European diseases such as typhoid and smallpox took even more Choctaw lives (Adair, 1775; Pesantubbee, 2005; Woods, 1978). Throughout the French settlement of Louisiana, the Choctaw were constant partners with the French. Ultimately, however, as a result of the Treaty of Paris of 1763, France lost most of its North American empire to England and Spain.

RELATIONS WITH THE ENGLISH

When the French lost the Seven Years War in 1763, the Choctaw were forced to deal with the English, who had previously sided with the Chickasaw to eliminate some of the French-allied competition (see, e.g., Nairne, 1708, cited in Peebles, 1983c). In addition to direct warfare, this had been attempted through financing Chickasaw and Muscogee slaving raids against Choctaw communities. Such behavior was justified through an English view of the Choctaw people concisely penned by James Adair (1775): "The general observation of the traders among them is just: who affirm them to be divested of every property of a human being, except shape and language" (p. 285).

Choctaw interaction with the English had been primarily through the English-backed traders who were involved in the deerskin and slave trades. Hudson (1976) lists estimates of deerskin export from 1699 to 1715 at an average of 54,000 per year; he also notes that when the French initiated a truce between the Chickasaw and the Choctaw in 1702, it was estimated that the Chickasaws had enslaved 500 Choctaws and killed 1,800 of them—all this at the instigation of the Carolina traders supported by the English.

Most of the interaction was bellicose. The Yamasee War of 1715 was a revolt by the Creek, Choctaw, and some Cherokees against the Carolina traders. The English managed to play the Cherokees against the Creeks, and the war ended in 1717 with a peace between the Carolinians and the Creeks. Other skirmishes occurred throughout the period, resulting in the greater interactions as a result of the French and Indian War (Seven Years War) of 1756–1763.

The Choctaws, like the other tribes in North America, were pawns in the European struggles for economic and military empires. Although the Choctaws were not markedly involved in military battles, they felt the impact of the War. With English victory, colonists moved into what had previously been French lands, thereby putting pressure on—and ultimately displacing—the tribes who had lived and hunted there. Two centuries' worth of economic relationships were destroyed (Unser, 1988), and the Choctaws had to learn to deal with new masters. King George's Proclamation of 1763, aimed at keeping colonists and Indians separated, was poorly enforced and met by the colonists with distaste. More and more colonists headed beyond the frontier in search of land and economic gain, claiming the land they had "won" in the war that the Indians had "lost."

CONCLUSION

At the time of European contact, the Choctaw were primarily family groups loosely affiliated with other groups who relied on corn-based agriculture, supplemented by hunting and gathering. They lived in huts built of upright logs with mud-plastered walls, and with raised cane-matted platforms along interior walls (Swanton, 1918). Their utensils were suitable for groups who moved frequently with the season, and consisted of earthenware pottery, baskets, skins, and other items manufactured of natural, easily available materials.

However, at the time of the War of Independence in 1776, the Choctaw were changed beyond belief. Woods (1978) rightly notes that interactions with Europeans and reliance on European trade goods totally altered the tribes:

> No longer did these Indians spend their winter months making bows and arrows, as had been their long-established custom, for they now relied on the musket for fighting and hunting. The skins of the deer and other animals that were killed were no longer used exclusively for clothing. Most of them were exchanged with the French traders for European goods. The Indians soon learned to prefer cotton cloth to skins for clothing, and brass and iron pots to pottery for cooking and other domestic purposes. The status of women, while enhanced because of their role in preparing hides for the "market," was reduced with the lessened emphasis on their ownership of the land as the economy became more directed to hunting than to farming. (pp. 375–376)

Choctaw relationships with the Americans derived from their involvement with the newly established United States of America after the conclusion of the Treaty of Paris in 1783, a prelude to the U.S. policy of removal and relocation of the 1830s.

3

❖

"A Nation Divided": Dancing Rabbit Creek and Removal

RELATIONS WITH THE UNITED STATES

English involvement with the Choctaw following the French and Indian War continued to be peripheral. After the signing of the Treaty of Paris in 1763, the English took over French trading contact with the Choctaw. The British Army maintained administration of the Choctaw up until the American Revolution (Karr, 1998/1999). When the Revolutionary War broke out, the tribe remained mostly neutral, even though a number of Choctaw warriors fought for the Colonies, as noted in Article 21 of the Dancing Rabbit Creek Treaty, and some supported the efforts of the English (Kappler, [1904] 1971). However, after the signing of the 1783 Treaty of Paris, the Choctaw, like the majority of American Indians, were all treated as defeated parties, regardless of whose side they fought on (O'Brien, 2001).

THE CONTINENTAL CONGRESS AND THE CHOCTAW

Official relations between the Choctaw and the United States began at the end of the Revolutionary War in 1786 with the signing of the Treaty of Hopewell on January 3, 1786 (DeRosier, 1970). After the American Revolutionary War, the United States gave tacit recognition to the rights of tribes to self-government by entering into treaties with the Indians as distinct political communities. The Treaty of Hopewell gave the government the right to establish three trading posts within Choctaw territory, fixed the boundaries of native land, and withdrew federal protection over any Europeans on tribal lands, purportedly to discourage European settlement on tribal lands (Painter-Thorne, 2008/2009).

The terms of the treaty consisted of 11 items: (1) The Choctaw were to restore prisoners, slaves, and property taken during the war; (2) the Choctaw agreed to be received into the "favor and protection of the United States of America" (Kappler, [1904] 1971, p. 12); (3) boundaries of the United States and Choctaw territories were defined; (4) no citizens of the United States were to settle on Indian lands, and Indians could punish violators as they pleased; (5) the Choctaw were to deliver to U.S. authorities criminals who committed robbery, murder, or capital crimes; (6) citizens of the United States who committed crimes against Indians were to be punished; (7) the Choctaw were to restrain from retaliation for offenses against them; (8) only the United States could enter into trade with Indians; (9) traders were to be allowed to enter Choctaw lands and towns and were to be protected from harm by the Choctaw; (10) the Choctaw were to give notice of any known designs against the United States by tribes or any person; and finally, (11) the Choctaw promised peace and friendship with the United States eternally.

The United States, in this regard, continued a process begun by the British of creating treaties with the tribes, but although the British were content to let the tribes generally operate independently, the U.S. government actively pursued a strategy of Indian assimilation and acculturation to white society, using its military to pursue this goal (Karr, 1998/1999). For the Choctaw, the growth of the United States was in direct competition with Choctaw expansion (Carson, 1997). The treaty, and the wane of European rivalries in the region, brought an end to the intertribal and imperial wars that had characterized a considerable part of the region throughout much of the eighteenth century.

Various aspects of the Treaty of Hopewell led to problems between the young United States and the Choctaw. The United States, for its part, failed to prevent squatters from impinging on Choctaw lands within the boundaries established by Article III of the Treaty. Because Article IV of the Treaty allowed the Choctaw to punish squatters "as they please," some Choctaw chose to punish squatters by raiding their settlements for cattle (Carson, 1997, p. 7). This created an issue for the United States as it struggled between protecting the property of U.S. citizens while also trying to live up to its treaty responsibilities.

Article VII of the Treaty attempted to do away with the tribal mechanism of justice entailed in "retaliation." One part of the Choctaw justice system provided that in the case of an injury against one party, the injured party gained justice "in kind"—by retaliating against the other party. Such retaliation ("blood feuds") often led to incessant feuding between parties, as each one tried to gain "justice" from the other.

Articles VIII and IX regulated trade between the Choctaw and the United States. Article VIII established that only the United States could regulate trade with the tribes (much like with other "foreign" countries); Article IX provided that the Choctaw would allow traders to enter into their country and be protected from theft and depredation.

Trade became the most powerful weapon of the United States. The Choctaw and the other tribes in the region relied so heavily on European manufactured goods that, by design, Jefferson suggested the Indians be allowed to "run into debt, because we observe that when these debts get beyond what the individual can pay, they become willing to lop them off by a cession of lands" (Sheehan, 1974, p. 171). The factory system also situated "a stable civilian federal presence near Indian country that could oversee trade, enforce regulations, report on rapidly changing situations, and promote social policy initiatives" (Rockwell, 2010, p. 88).

The Choctaw settled into an uneasy relationship with the United States following the Treaty of Hopewell. The period was a time of unrest for European nations, however, as the Napoleonic Wars in Europe played out. The Choctaw got drawn into the political conflict after the United States negotiated the Treaty of Fort Adams with the Choctaw in 1801 for the cession of Choctaw land to serve as a buffer against a possible Napoleonic invasion from New Orleans.

The United States, in response to British trade restrictions and other actions related to the Napoleonic Wars, declared war against the British and its American Indian allies in 1812. The Indians, organized loosely in support of the English, were under the leadership of the Shawnee warrior Tecumseh.

As a prelude to the War of 1812, in 1811, the Shawnee warrior Tecumseh traveled to the southern tribes to try to convince them to side with the English against the American colonies (Whicker, 1922). Pushmataha spoke against such an alliance, and the Choctaw expelled Tecumseh from their nation when he tried to enlist them in his Indian confederacy. Ultimately, the Choctaw fought alongside American forces against the Red Stick faction of the Creeks, who had chosen to join Tecumseh's alliance at the Battle of Horseshoe Bend in 1814 (Baird, 1973). The Choctaw war chief Pushmataha led 800 Choctaw troops, who became a part of General Andrew Jackson's army.

Choctaw war chief Pushmataha, by 19th-century American painter Charles Bird King. Pushmataha died in Washington, D.C., and was buried with full military honors at the Congressional Cemetery there. (McKenney, Thomas L. and James Hall. *The Indian Tribes of North America*, 1836–1844)

While the battles with the Creeks were going on, British troops landed in the Chesapeake Bay area in 1814 and marched toward Washington. The U.S. military forces were badly routed, and the British burned the Capitol and the White House, along with most of nonresidential Washington.

The British pressed onward toward Baltimore. They bombarded Fort McHenry, which guarded Baltimore's harbor, but were unable to take it. This event inspired Francis Scott Key to write "The Star-Spangled Banner." Unsuccessful at Baltimore, Cochrane's damaged fleet limped to Jamaica for repairs and made preparations for an invasion of New Orleans, hoping to cut off American use of the Mississippi River.

The signing of the Treaty of Ghent on December 24, 1814, officially ended the war, returning U.S.–Britain relations to the same status as they had been before the war. In New Orleans, British troops engaged Andrew Jackson's army at the Battle of New Orleans. Pushmataha led Choctaw troops against the British in support of Jackson's army at the Battle of New Orleans, and again in 1816, Choctaw warriors fought alongside the U.S. troops in the Creek War. Despite Choctaw loyalty, the United States demanded further land cessions in 1816. John Swanton ([1931] 2001) notes that the Choctaw were never at war with the United States, although some Choctaw individuals sided with Tecumseh.

Even though this battle had been fought unnecessarily (the treaty was already signed), the United States celebrated wildly, manifesting an upsurge in American nationalism and pushing William Henry Harrison, James Tyler, and Andrew Jackson into the national political spotlight.

In spite of the Choctaw support for the American cause against the English, however, Choctaw borders were plagued with illegal immigrants coming from the United States. By design, the Choctaw fell into debt to U.S. trading companies (DeRosier, 1970; Perdue, 1988) and were forced to concede portions of their land to settle outstanding debts. The Choctaw were forced to give up more sections of land, and via Article IV of the Treaty of Doak's Stand in 1820, they agreed to boundaries that were to "remain without alteration until the period at which said nation shall become so civilized and enlightened as to be made citizens of the United States" (Kappler, [1904] 1971, p. 192).

A party of 10 Choctaws, led by Apukshunubbee, Pushmataha, and Moshulatubbee—the three principle leaders of the Choctaw—along with David Folsom, Nitakechi, & Robert Cole, among others—journeyed to Washington City (the name for Washington, DC, at the time) to make their case for protection and to ask that the white trespassers encroaching on tribal lands be removed. On the way to Washington, Apukshunubbee died from a broken neck suffered purportedly as the result of a fall from a hotel balcony, although other stories said he fell from a cliff. Washington authorities tacitly recognized Robert Cole as chief when they presented him the medal of friendship that was to have been given to Apukshunubbee. Pushmataha died of the "croup" while the delegation was in Washington, although some historians have suggested that the sizeable hotel and bar bills indicated other possibilities (Debo, [1934] 1961).

The 1825 Treaty of Washington City provided options for the Choctaw to stay in Mississippi, in addition to financial annuities for the Tribe. It also resulted in the cession of lands in what was then Arkansas Territory, relinquishment of a Choctaw debt, and the creation of an agent and blacksmith for the Choctaws west of the Mississippi.

However, with the election of Andrew Jackson as president in 1828, the Choctaw leaders recognized that removal was inevitable. Choctaw leadership was in disarray, with conflicting loyalties and allegiances arising due to the conflicts (O'Brien, 2008). Moshulatubbee supported removal, yet he championed traditional rights. He prevented the western division leader Greenwood LeFlore from naming himself chief of the entire Choctaws in early 1830 (O'Brien, 2001). Greenwood LeFlore, with a French father and a Choctaw mother, chose European education for his children and full participation in the plantation economy of Mississippi.

PRE-REMOVAL CHOCTAW TOWN SYSTEM

From at least the eighteenth century, there existed among the Choctaws three principal geographic and political divisions: the western (Okla Falaya) district, the eastern (Okla Tannip or Okla Tanap) district, and the Six Towns (or Okla Hanali) divisions. The western division villages were scattered around the upper Pearl River watershed; the eastern division towns were located around the upper Chickasawhay River and lower Tombigbee River watersheds; and the Six Towns were distributed along the upper Leaf River and mid-Chickasawhay River watersheds.

These divisions reflected the diverse ethnic origins and makeup of the Choctaws. Originally, the Choctaws were separate societies located throughout east-central Mississippi and west-central Alabama. These independent societies first joined together sometime after 1540 (when Hernando De Soto's expedition ravaged the Southeast with disease) and before 1699 (when the French arrived on the Gulf Coast). Each district maintained its own group of chiefs and other leaders well into the nineteenth century.

At the time of removal, Nitakechi was chief of the Six Towns; Apukshunubbee was chief of the Okla Falaya; and Moshulatubbee was chief of the Okla Tannip. During removal, the three districts moved to and settled in Oklahoma Territory, generally in proximity to the other towns of their Mississippi districts. These districts, named after famous chiefs of the districts in Mississippi, were the Moshulatubbee district in the north, the Apukshunubbee district in the southeastern one-third of the nation, and the Pushmataha district in the southwestern one-third of the nation.

THE TREATY OF DANCING RABBIT CREEK

Shortly after Jackson's election, Georgia, Alabama, Mississippi, and Tennessee tried to bring the Indians who lived inside their borders under their jurisdiction (Young, 1958). In 1829 and 1830, Mississippi passed resolutions (against federal law) that declared unceded Choctaw lands "state property," and "terminated" Choctaw sovereignty, thereby making Choctaw communities subject to the state's laws and possible attack by the militia (Hudson, 1976). Tribesmen were threatened with subjection to mustering with the militia, working on roads, and paying taxes. Some of the states established county governments within the tribal domains and, in some cases, gave legal protection to purchasers of Indian improvements. The states even threatened punishment to any person who might attempt to deter another from signing a removal treaty or enrolling for emigration. The object of these laws was to destroy the tribal governments and to thrust upon individual Indians the uncongenial alternative of adjusting to the burdens of state citizenship or removing beyond state jurisdiction (Young, 1958). On September 27, 1830, under these continual threats, and bolstered by the fear of forced removal (Satz, 1986), Choctaw chiefs Moshulatubbee and Greenwood LeFlore, against the wishes of the majority (Claiborne, 1880), ceded the last of the homeland in the Treaty of Dancing Rabbit Creek.

The instigation for the Treaty was the Indian Removal Act, passed by Congress on May 28, 1830. The Act provided for "an exchange of lands with the Indians residing in any of the states or territories, and for their removal west of the river Mississippi." The Jackson administration presented removal as a means of protecting the tribes within state boundaries. In an April 1829 letter to the Cherokees, Secretary of War John Eaton implied Indians were merely "occupants" of sovereign states (Bowes, 2014, p. 74). Removal as a political ambition was tied to Manifest Destiny—the need to expand American territory from one coast to another—and American Indians stood in the way. But it was also more: Lyons expands on this idea, stating that "while the original political policy was concerned with actual physical removals like the Trail of Tears, the underlying ideology of removal in its own way justified and encouraged the systematic losses of Indian life: the removal of livelihood and language, the removal of security and self-esteem, the removal of religion and respect" (Lyons, 2010, p. 8). Thus, even though the Choctaw were being hurried toward "American civilization," they were viewed as standing in American civilization's path in its march to the Pacific.

The Treaty provided for several types of allotments for the Choctaw who intended to relocate rather than remain in Mississippi on their own property. Special reservations were given to the chiefs and their numerous family connections as a means of sweetening the relocation process. Greenwood LeFlore chose to stay in Mississippi on his plantation rather than removing to Indian Territory, because of the generous reward he received in the removal document (Clark, 2009).

Government officials made arrangements for up to 1,600 allotments of 80 to 480 acres—based on the size of the current owner's farm—to be offered to those who intended to leave. In theory, the government intended the Choctaw to get the property they lived on in Mississippi "allotted" to them, and then for the Choctaw landowners to sell them to private persons or to the government as a means to pay off their debts and to help finance their resettlement and new activities in the West (Satz, 1986). In this manner, the government thought the landowners might get the maximum price for their improvements.

The right to sell the allotments was useful to the Choctaw landowners who were accustomed to operating in the upper realms of American economic culture. Many of them received handsome payment for their allotments, whereas other chose to keep part of their holdings and remain in Mississippi. Many of the landowners who benefited from the sale of their allotments were mixed-bloods, but the less cosmopolitan full-bloods were often taken advantage of.

When the process of allotting lands to individuals began, speculators loaned whisky, muslin, horses, slaves, and other useful commodities to the "new" property owner. In return, the speculators received the written promise of the borrower to sell his allotment to them as soon as its boundaries were defined. Generally the speculators located their client's allotments on "desirable" lands. Often, the speculators sold their "interest" in the lands to men of capital (Young, 1958).

Even though the lifestyles of the Choctaw had been forever changed by the influence of European products and cultural acculturation, nothing impacted them as drastically as the 1830 Treaty of Dancing Rabbit Creek. Many of the Choctaws who voluntarily migrated to Indian Territory (an area carved out of land within Quapaw, Caddo, and Wichita tribal territory) prior to the forced migrations were those who were less established in the homeland. As a result, the early arrivals in Indian Territory were able to choose the best lands for framing, hunting, and habitation. Those who arrived last—those with the most to lose by leaving their developed properties in Mississippi—were forced to choose from areas less favorable for farming or grazing activities. Thus, in many ways, economic and social structures were overturned by the removal process, and it took a while for the Choctaw culture to recover.

According to explicit provision in Article 14 of the Treaty, Choctaw individuals could register with the Mississippi Indian agent, become U.S. citizens, and continue to live in Mississippi on allotted land of their choice. At the end of five years' residence, those who received these allotments were to have fee simple title to their lands and become citizens. It was expected that approximately 200 persons would take land under this article. After the Treaty's ratification, the local Indian agent, William Ward, simply refused to register the people who came to him (Claiborne, 1880; Satz, 1986). If individuals were not registered to remain, they had to move to Indian Territory.

Those who chose to remain in Mississippi were denied a great deal of the promises made to them, and only about 1,300 of the Choctaws who stayed were given the parcels of land that had been guaranteed by the Treaty. Wolfe (1987) notes how communication hindered much of the organization necessary to bring people in for conversations. Additionally, the Six Towns Choctaw met in council and approached Ward with lists of names of those who wished to remain. Ward destroyed or discarded the lists.

By 1850, virtually none of the Choctaw who had been given reservations of land in Mississippi still retained them, having been systematically swindled out of them or simply forced off the land by unscrupulous white settlers. Many went to Oklahoma, but many still stayed on, unwilling to leave their homeland. The ones who stayed eked out a meager existence throughout the rest of the nineteenth century by living off the land and by becoming tenant farmers and sharecroppers on land that had once been theirs (Carleton, 2002).

REMOVAL

Grant Foreman, in the preface of his book *Indian Removal: The Emigration of the Five Civilized Tribes of Indians* (1976), noted that "it is doubtful if white people with their readier adaptability can understand the sense of grief and desolation that overwhelmed the Indians when they were compelled to leave . . . and begin the long sad journey toward the setting sun which they called the Trail of Tears." He goes on to say that the "woeful mismanagement and cruel and unnecessary suffering by the emigrants" was due to a general ineptitude and lack of experience by the political appointees charged with dealing with the Choctaw, and closes with saying, "Much suffering, perhaps, was inevitable, but much would have been prevented by considerate and skillful preparation."

Probably most people who have heard of "Removal" associate the suffering of the tribal members with the Cherokee who were forced out of Georgia and other states in the east. However, the Choctaws were the first Indians to be removed as a nation by the U.S. government, to new land in the West.

The first movement of the Choctaws from their homelands east of the Mississippi River began as a result of the 1825 Treaty of Washington City, whereby the Choctaw ceded about one-fourth of the lands given to them by the Treaty of Doak's Stand five years earlier. Some Choctaw voluntarily migrated to the lands promised to them under the treaties, but found there were people already occupying the lands. The federal government failed to remove those who had occupied the land, and the Choctaw migrants who did try to settle in these lands "had settled on Choctaw land on the Red River" away from the white squatters (Bearss, 1969).

By the end of 1830, Choctaw began moving to Indian Territory. The first group to head to the West was composed of about 400 Choctaw captains and high-ranking individuals. These people had sold their Mississippi hold-ings lands out of fear that if they delayed selling, the land values would decrease as more and more property became available.

The first of the government-sponsored removals started in 1831. Dur-ing this first year, 15 percent of the then 20,000-member Choctaw tribe left for their new homeland (Lambert, 2007a). Administered by the new Bureau of Indian Affairs, the journey was ill financed and ill supplied. About 4,000 emigrants were transported by steamboat from Memphis, Vicksburg, or Natchez as far as possible up the Arkansas and Ouachita Rivers. Once they disembarked in Arkansas Territory, they walked the rest of the way to Indian Territory. They arrived at their new homes after a five-month jour-ney, sick, exhausted, and discouraged.

In 1832, about 9,000 Choctaws were removed, but this time most were forced to walk all the way. Because the first removal was deemed by the government to have been too expensive, the remaining removals were turned over to the U.S. Army. Rations were decreased, and transportation was provided only for the very young and those who were very sick. Addi-tionally, one of the worse blizzards in the history of that region occurred during the winter of 1831–1832 (Debo, [1934] 1961), causing great loss of life and suffering among the emigrants.

The weather was less of a problem during the final removal in 1833, but the emigrants faced other hardships. A cholera epidemic swept down the Mississippi and caught those who were crossing. In addition, they were forced to cross unsettled country of vast swamps, dense forests, impenetra-ble canebrakes, and swollen rivers. By the end of the last removal in 1833, the Choctaw were mostly in Indian Territory.

Estimates for the number of Choctaw who died on the removals vary. Lambert (2007a) writes that, by 1843, "only 12,690 Choctaws lived in Indian Territory, a reflection of the high number who died on the perilous and poorly organized trek that was later termed the Trail of Tears" (p. 40). Some estimates based on muster roles and agent's notes indicate that perhaps as many as 2,500 Choctaws died during the 1832 removal alone.

By all accounts, the Choctaws endured unimaginable suffering and hard-ship on the Trail of Tears (Debo, [1934] 1961; DeRosier, 1970; Foreman, 1976; Gibson, 1965; Lambert, 2007a). Many aspects of the journey were long and hard. Some parties were forced to walk 30 miles in waist-deep swamp water, and some endured near-blizzard conditions. Nearly all experienced an inadequate supply of food, blankets, and horses with which to carry the sick, elders, and youth.

Regardless of the actual numbers, the population of the tribe was deci-mated by the losses sustained during this terrible experience. The deaths

Native Americans travel the Trail of Tears in a forced migration to land set aside by the Indian Removal Act of 1830. It is estimated that between 1836 and 1839, 2,500 of the 11,500 Choctaws who started the journey died along the way. (North Wind Picture Archives)

were not spread evenly over all generations and age groups, as the old and the young were unable or unprepared for the rigors of the marches. The deaths of the elders led to a great loss of traditional knowledge and family histories; the death of the youth created a generation chasm that took time to refill. Additionally, communities collapsed as families took different routes and arrived at different times.

Those who remained in Mississippi soon learned that the allotments they were promised were hard to come by. Influenced by some of the Choctaw leaders, such as Greenwood LeFlore (who had profited by his actions in negotiating the Treaty), it is estimated that about 4,000 Choctaw chose to accept allotments and come under the jurisdiction of the State of Mississippi rather than move to Indian Territory.

Numerous authors such as DeRosier (1970), Osburn (2016), Peterson (1972, 1987), and Wolfe (1987) have documented some of the issues the Mississippi Indians faced in trying to gain or retain their lands following the Treaty of Dancing Rabbit Creek. The Treaty provided three provisions for

---

TRAIL OF TEARS (AND OKLAHOMA CHOCTAW TRAIL OF TEARS WALK)

The "Trail of Tears" is a generalized term given to the series of removals of American Indian tribes from their homelands in the southeastern United States to Indian Territory. The forced relocations were carried out by government authorities following the passage of the Indian Removal Act in 1830. Many of the relocated people suffered from exposure, disease, and starvation on the journeys to their new lands, and many died before reaching their destinations. The most notable forced removals included members of the Cherokee, Muscogee (Creek), Seminole, Chickasaw, and Choctaw nations. The phrase "Trail of Tears" originates from a description of the removal of many Native American tribes, including the infamous Cherokee Nation relocation in 1838.

The Choctaw emigrated in three stages: the first in the fall of 1831, the second in 1832, and the last in 1833. The first wave of removal suffered the most, whereas the second and third waves experienced fewer hardships than the others. Removal continued throughout the 19th century. In 1846, 1,000 Choctaw were removed, and by 1930, only 1,665 remained in Mississippi.

Nearly 15,000 Choctaws, together with 1,000 slaves, made the move to Indian Territory (later Oklahoma) in three migrations between 1831 and 1833, including the devastating winter blizzard of 1830–1831 and the cholera epidemic of 1832. Although there is no accurate number of those who died along the march, it is estimated that 2,500 of the 11,500 Choctaws who started the journey died.

Each year in May, the Choctaw Nation of Oklahoma commemorates the Trail of Tears with a 2.5-mile Trail of Tears Walk and Heritage Day at Tuskahoma, Oklahoma. After the walk, events include a short program, cultural demonstrations such as basket weaving and pottery making, stickball, and traditional Choctaw dancing. Other events also highlight Choctaw culture.

---

land allotments in Mississippi: first, to the various men (such as LeFlore) whose services, needs, or influences deserved reward; second, under Article 14, to individuals who chose to remain in Mississippi under the jurisdiction of the state; and third, under Article 19, to heads of families on land located around their "improvements," determined in relation to the land under cultivation.

Most of the people who actually benefitted from these arrangements were those such as Greenwood LeFlore who had already been a part of the American economy. These owners of large plantations were accustomed to selling their crops and hiring labor, and their experience in negotiating treaties also gave them the ability to better bargain over the price of lands. Many of these landowners sold their allotments for fair value. Some kept part of their holdings and remained in Alabama and Mississippi as planters, practicing as land speculators on the side.

Others, such as the more traditional Choctaws, were unaccustomed to the idea of land tenure, land sales, and land speculation. Many of those who chose to stay struggled to obtain the land due to them. Agent Ward stymied many of them through his actions, and others saw their homes and improvements destroyed or stolen from them (Debo, [1934] 1961; Peterson, 1987, p. 3).

Those who did receive their allotments often suffered at the hands of land speculators who made loans of whisky, muslin, horses, slaves, and other useful commodities to the new property owner. In exchange, the speculator received the Indian's written promise to sell his allotment to them once it was legally his to sell. Speculators often turned around and sold their "interest" in the lands to men of capital rather than wait for the sale. Government agents supported this sort of arrangement because it was felt that the individual Indians should have their profit in order to help them remove to Indian Territory. Unfortunately, this sort of speculation in Indian lands led to frauds that impoverished the Indians, soiled the reputation of the government, and actually delayed the emigration of the tribes (Young, 1958).

As a result of the land speculation and unscrupulous dealing, most of those who were allotted land lost it and were left landless. Many of them faced the alternative of emigration or destitution; some chose to emigrate, whereas others chose to remain. Those who stayed were forced to survive as "Mississippi Indians" under state laws.

Thus, the Treaty of Dancing Rabbit Creek did what the Spanish, French, and English could not do—divide and "conquer" the Choctaw.

NOTABLE FIGURES

Pre-Removal Chiefs

The three pre-Removal chiefs of the Choctaw were Apukshunubbee, Moshulatubbee, and Pushmataha.

Apukshunubbee (ca. 1740–October 18, 1824), also spelled Apvkshvnvbbee, Apʊkshʊnʊbbee, Puckshenubbee, Pushunnubbu, and Pukshunnubbee, was one of the three principal chiefs of the Choctaw in the early 1800s. Apukshunubbee led the western Okla Falaya ("Tall People") District in what is now Madison County in Mississippi. During the early nineteenth century, Apukshunubbee, along with two other division chiefs, negotiated and signed several treaties with the U.S. government, hoping to end the encroachment on Choctaw land by ceding territory to settlers. In 1824, Apukshunubbee headed to Washington, DC, with Moshulatubbee and Pushmataha, two division chiefs, to meet with U.S. officials; he died en route, in Maysville, Kentucky, after suffering a fall.

Moshulatubbee (ca. 1750–1770–c. 1838), also spelled Mosholetvbbi, AmoshuliTvbi, Musholatubbee, Moshaleh Tubbee, and Mushulatubba, was the chief of the Choctaw Okla Tannap ("Lower Towns"), one of three major Choctaw divisions in the early nineteenth century. At the time of removal, Moshulatubbee lead the tribe to Indian Territory after being elected principal chief. In 1812, Moshulatubbee, along with his warriors, assisted General Andrew Jackson in the Creek Wars against Creek Red Sticks. He led Choctaw warriors in a fight against the British in 1815 at the Battle of New Orleans.

In December 1824, Moshulatubbee, representing the Choctaw as one of three principal chiefs, led a delegation to Washington, seeking help against the intrusion of European-American settlers. Moshulatubbee signed the Treaty of Dancing Rabbit Creek on September 26, 1830, which ceded most of the remaining Choctaw territory in Alabama and Mississippi to the U.S. government in exchange for land in Indian Territory.

Pushmataha (born ca. 1764, died December 30, 1824), was the chief of the Choctaw "Six Towns" (or southern) Division of the Choctaw tribal town system. Sometime around 1800, Pushmataha became a leading chief and began playing a major role in negotiations with other peoples, especially the Americans. In 1811, he convinced the Choctaw warriors to side with the United States rather than with Tecumseh's Indian confederation. In 1815, he again led Choctaw warriors against the British in the Battle of New Orleans.

Along with Apukshunubbee and Moshulatubbee, Pushmataha traveled to Washington City in 1824. During the 1824 negotiations, Pushmataha became sick and died. He was buried with full military honors in the Congressional Cemetery in Washington, DC.

4

❖

New Structures: Post-Removal Choctaw Developments

FORMING THE NATION

The Choctaw who chose to travel to the western lands in Indian Territory took their tripartite division of government and territory with them (Kidwell, 2004). Immediately after the Choctaw arrived in Indian Territory, they began forming their new government and internal governing structure. The Choctaws adopted a new constitution in 1834, creating a national council of nine elected members from each of the three districts, and three district chiefs (Clark, 2009). The district chiefs were regarded as ex officio members of the Council, and any two of them could veto legislative enactments unless they were repassed by a two-thirds majority (Debo, [1934] 1961). The districts were named after their three pre-Removal chiefs Moshulatubbee, Apukshunubbee, and Pushmataha: Moshulatubbee in the north, the Pushmataha west of the Kiamichi, and the Apukshunubbee in the southeast (Kidwell, 2004).

The Moshulatubbee District, also called the First District, encompassed the northern one-third of the nation. The District's administrative seat of government was Gaines Court House, which also doubled as the county seat of Gaines County. The courthouse was northeast of modern-day McAlester, Oklahoma. Included in the Moshulatubbee District were the Choctaw counties of Gaines, Sans Bois, Skullyville, Sugar Loaf, and Tobucksy.

Apukshunubbee District, also called the Second District, encompassed the southeastern one-third of the nation. Its administrative seat of government was Alikchi, in Nashoba County, Choctaw Nation. Alikchi is located east of present-day Rattan, Oklahoma, and north of Wright City, Oklahoma, in McCurtain County. Included in the Apukshunubbee District were the Choctaw Nation counties of Bok Tuklo, Cedar, Eagle, Nashoba, Red River, Towson, and Wade.

The Pushmataha District, also called the Third District, encompassed the southwestern one-third of the nation, west of the Kiamichi River. The Pushmataha District's final and most important administrative seat of government was Mayhew, Indian Territory, a former Presbyterian missionary station two miles north of the present-day Boswell, Oklahoma. Included in the Pushmataha District were the Choctaw Nation counties of Atoka, Jack's Fork, Blue, Jackson, and Kiamitia (Kiamichi).

The lighthorsemen, who had been established in the Treaty of Doak's Stand, constituted the enforcement arm of the government, and courts and laws supplanted the traditional system of retaliation between families (Choctaw Nation, 1838; Kidwell, 2004).

In 1837, in response to the Choctaw removal, the Chickasaw tried to find a place in the Indian Territory for themselves. The Choctaws agreed to lease part of their territory to the Chickasaw Tribe, which sold its land to the United States in the Treaty of Pontotoc in 1832. By the time the Chickasaw entered into the treaty, all the land in Indian Territory was committed to other Indian nations. The Choctaw-Chickasaw Treaty of 1837 guaranteed the Chickasaws a home in the western part of the Choctaw Nation (perhaps to serve as a buffer against the plains Indians) and assimilated them politically as a fourth district in a revised constitution promulgated in 1838 (Choctaw Nation, 1838; Clark, 2009; Kappler, [1904] 1971; Kidwell, 2004).

In 1842, the unicameral legislature that had been established in 1834 was replaced by a bicameral legislative branch, with a Senate of four members from each district holding office for two years. The House of Representatives were elected annually and based on population (Debo, [1934] 1961). After 1850, a system of county, circuit, and supreme courts comprised the tribe's judicial branch (Lambert, 2007a).

The Chickasaws, who had been integrated into the Choctaw system of governance by the constitution of 1838, regained their political and financial independence under the terms of the constitution of 1855. In spite of this, the Choctaw and the Chickasaw continued to share a legal interest in the entire territory throughout the remainder of the nineteenth century and up until the 1970s (Lambert, 2007a).

From their arrival in Indian Territory and up until the Civil War, the Choctaw government developed, modeled after the U.S. system of governance. The population flourished as well. With the majority of the Choctaw population spread over the eastern half of the Choctaw-Chickasaw territory, those settled along the larger valleys of the Arkansas and Red River valleys turned to cotton cultivation (Doran, 1975). Some of these planters created "mansion-style dwellings" on their plantations (Lambert, 2007a).

Many of the Choctaw who came to Oklahoma brought with them the slaves they had held, and the numbers continued to increase as the Choctaws more fully entered into the market economy. By 1860, the number of

---

CHOCTAW ACADEMIES IN OKLAHOMA

"Civilizing" American Indians was a main objective of the U.S. government in the nineteenth century. This policy was supported by American churches, such as the Baptist, Methodist, and Presbyterian, which desired to help Indians assimilate and become Christians. Churches accomplished this by sending missionaries to the tribes. As a result of this activity, several mission schools were started among the Choctaw in Mississippi, beginning in 1818.

After Removal to Indian Territory, missionaries developed neighborhood schools for the Choctaw children. In 1842, the Choctaw General Council established six boarding schools: Spencer Academy, Fort Coffee Academy, Koonaha (Kunaha or Sunsha) Female Seminary, Ianubbee (Ayanubbe) Female Seminary, Chuwahla (Chuwalla) Female Seminary, and Wheelock Female Seminary. Fort Coffee Academy was divided into male and female branches in 1845 with the creation of New Hope Seminary. In 1845, Armstrong Academy was established near present Bokchito in Bryan County, and in 1846, Norwalk Academy was opened near Wheelock Seminary as a boarding school for boys. Missionaries originally ran these institutions, but by the 1890s those that remained open were operated by educated Choctaws.

The Civil War had a disastrous effect on the Choctaw boarding schools. All were closed for the duration of the conflict. After the war, the boarding schools were slowly reestablished. As more boarding schools were needed, the Choctaw General Council organized three additional facilities in December 1891. The Curtis Act of 1898 put all Choctaw Nation schools under U.S. government control. The boarding schools continued to operate, but one by one they were closed. By 1930, only Jones Academy and Wheelock Seminary remained, and Wheelock was merged with Jones in 1955. Jones Academy is presently maintained under the direction of the Choctaw Nation as a residential care center for elementary and secondary school age children. Youths residing there attend the Hartshorne public schools.

slaves in Choctaw country totaled more than 2,300, approximately 14 percent of the entire population (Doran, 1975).

Throughout this time as well, the Choctaw education system developed. Most of the classes were conducted in English, primarily through the actions of missionaries. Portions of the Old Testament and the entire New Testament were published in the Choctaw language. Debo observes that "in 1837 the number of tracts published in the Choctaw language during the year reached a total of 30,500, embracing 576,000 pages" (Debo, [1934] 1961, p. 62). In her analysis of the Choctaw education system, Debo rightfully ties its development to the Christian missionaries. She notes the role of missionaries of the American Board of Commissioners for Foreign Missions; the Methodist and Presbyterian missionaries; and the actions of the Baptist missionaries.

By 1838, the Choctaw had eight "neighborhood" schools. Soon, "academies" were established at Goodland, Fort Coffee, Spencer, and Armstrong for the best male students, and female students received their further educational opportunities at seminaries at Goodwater, Pine Ridge, Wheelock, and New Hope (Gibson, 1965; Debo, [1934] 1961; Lambert, 2007a).

The tribal schools were under the control of a board of trustees—one member from each district, appointed by the district chiefs. Trustees were responsible for the neighborhood schools in their districts. They also were responsible for the appointment of the teachers. The board as a whole made contracts with missionary societies for the operation of the boarding schools. An act passed in 1853 provided for a Superintendent of Schools, who served as ex officio president of the board. Both the superintendent and the trustees were elected by the General Council for a four-year term.

THE MISSISSIPPI INDIANS

Those Choctaw who chose to remain in Mississippi continued to live on the margins of society. The Mississippi Constitution of 1832 gave the state the right to "admit to all the rights and privileges of free white citizens of the State to all such persons of the Choctaw and Chickasaw tribe of Indians as shall choose to remain in this state upon such terms as the legislature may from time to time deem proper." Thus, Mississippi was able to assert state jurisdiction over the Choctaws who remained in substitution for federal jurisdiction. Many of these Choctaw settled around the homes of leaders who had gained land as a result of their military service. These settlements were comprised of Choctaw speakers who "held Choctaw dances and stickball games, and lived under the authority of their *mingoes*," or town chiefs (Osburn, 2016, p. 203).

Louisiana Indians Walking Along a Bayou, by Alfred Boisseau (1847). The Jena Band of Choctaw Indians has incorporated the central figures of Boisseau's painting into the design of their tribal flag. (The Picture Art Collection/Alamy Stock Photo)

As late as the 1840s, an estimated 5,000 to 6,000 Choctaws remained in Mississippi. As the possibilities of retaining land or property vanished, most gradually accepted the inevitability of removal and departed for Oklahoma (Peterson, 1987). Wolfe (1987) noted, "In the four-year period 1845–1849, 5,120 Choctaws left Mississippi. Another 600 individuals migrated during 1853–1854. By 1860, only 1,000 Choctaws persistently remained in the state" (p. 13).

One example, that of Choctaw *mingo* Samuel Cobb, is telling. Cobb and his followers were located within Leake County, Mississippi, when pressured to relocate to Indian Territory in 1842. The community utilized "rituals of diplomacy between sovereign nations," but Cobb was unable to prevent state officials from invoking the 1830 citizenship law and dispossessing him of his property (Osburn, 2016, p. 207).

The remaining Choctaw avoided removal by remaining as squatters on less desirable land unoccupied by white settlers, forming a small minority in a society dominated by whites and composed largely of whites and blacks. As Peterson noted (1972), the Choctaw constantly struggled to maintain their separate ethnic communities. Prior to Reconstruction, Choctaws were non-white, but also non-slave. Their liminal position as neither white land-owner nor landless black impacted their ability to participate in the institutions of the dominant society that required them to either accept the

---

RELATIONS WITH IRELAND

In 1847, at the height of Ireland's Great Famine, Choctaws of Oklahoma gathered together funds and sent a donation of $170 as part of a wider action for the relief of the starving poor of Ireland. Despite the fact that the Choctaw had been uprooted from their homelands in Mississippi and forced to relocate to Oklahoma Territory only 16 years earlier, the Choctaw people pooled their money to send to Ireland. The selflessness of the Choctaw Nation still is taught in Irish schools, with an emphasis on the fact that they gave even when they couldn't afford to do so.

In 2015, Irish artist Alex Pentek constructed *Kindred Spirits,* an empty bowl made up of nine 20-foot-tall steel eagle feathers arranged in a circle. The sculpture is in commemoration of the Choctaw's gift and serves as a reminder of the relationship the Choctaws have developed with the Irish. In 1990, Choctaw leaders traveled to County Mayo to take part in a reenactment of an 1848 protest. The gesture was returned in 1992, when Irish leaders took part in a trek from Oklahoma to Mississippi. Former Irish President Mary Robinson also has been named an honorary Choctaw chief. Choctaw Chief Gary Batton and other Choctaw tribal members attended the 2015 unveiling of Pentek's sculpture in Bailic Park, Midleton, Cork County, Ireland.

---

position of "slave" or acquire land and be accepted as "white." Thus, because of this untenable positioning, those who remained in Mississippi did so in almost total social isolation until the end of the slave system.

THE CHOCTAW AND THE CIVIL WAR

Early Confederate victories in Indian Territory resulted in the capture of the federally controlled Fort Cobb, Fort Arbuckle, Fort Washita, and Fort Smith in Arkansas. With the Confederate states of Arkansas to the east, Texas to the south, and other tribes loyal to the Confederacy to the north, the Choctaw were in the midst of Confederate-held lands.

The Choctaw signed a treaty with the American Confederacy on May 7, 1861, justifying the action on the idea that the Confederacy appeared to offer the Tribe the best chance of maintaining its autonomy (Champagne, 1992). Choctaw economic ties and the Tribe's foundations in the American South all but ensured Choctaw participation with the Confederacy.

The Choctaws saw their first action in the 1861 campaign against the Union loyalist forces under Creek Chief Opothleyahola. In the Battles of Round Mountain and Chusto-Talasah (Bird Creek) during November and December of 1861, Albert Pike's Indian Brigade and Confederate Texas troops from Fort Smith defeated and pushed loyalist forces into Kansas (Cottrell, 1998; Milligan, 2003).

By September and October of 1862, Choctaw forces under the command of Douglas Cooper were involved in the Battle of Newtonia in Missouri before retreating back to Indian Territory. Cooper's rout at the Battle of Old Fort Wayne in October led to the retreat of the Indian Brigade to Skully-ville in Choctaw Territory (Cottrell, 1998; Milligan, 2003). Several more regiments and battalions were formed by the Choctaws. These units engaged in skirmishes and battles around eastern Indian Territory as well as Missouri and Arkansas. They were included within Albert Pike's Indian Brigade in 1861, which was later commanded by Cooper in 1862 (Spring, 2011).

The most important engagement of the war in Indian Territory was in July, 1863, at the Battle of Honey Springs (also called Elk Creek), the largest battle in Indian Territory. The federal troops defeated Cooper and forced him and the Indian Brigade back into the Choctaw Nation. With their victory, Union forces occupied all of Indian Territory north of the Canadian River and soon captured Fort Smith. Cooper's defeat at the Battle of Perryville in August of the same year led to the loss of his supply depot at Perryville; Little Rock in Arkansas was occupied in September (Cottrell, 1998; Milligan, 2003).

Choctaw forces continued to participate in Confederate battles and skirmishes throughout 1864, but the Civil War ended for the Choctaw Nation in June 1865. By means of the Treaty of 1866, the Choctaw Nation gave up one-third of its western land to the United States to be used to provide space for more tribes to be settled into Indian Territory. The Treaty also called for the tribe to permit the construction of a north–south and an east–west railroad through Choctaw country, which allowed for more white settlers to enter into Indian Territory and Choctaw lands (Spring, 2011).

The Civil War had a devastating impact on the Choctaw. In addition to the amount of land given up by the Treaty of 1866, Choctaws experienced the destruction of substantial amounts of their personal property, a temporary but prolonged closure of their schools, and the loss of possibly as much as 24 percent of their population (Debo, [1934] 1961; Kidwell, 2004; Lambert, 2007a). The Treaty also called for the tribe to grant citizenship to their freedmen over the objections of most Choctaws, who wanted the freedmen removed from their territory, and also over the objections of the majority of freedmen, who did not want to be under Choctaw jurisdiction (Champagne, 1992; Debo, [1934] 1961; Lambert, 2007a).

After the Civil War, emancipation and the presence of railroads through the Choctaw Nation led to massive immigration of invited and uninvited whites into the tribe's homeland. Without slaves to work the farms, Choctaws used white farm laborers from neighboring states. After the mid-1870s, these white laborers "raised most of the cotton grown on Choctaw lands" (Lambert, 2007a, p. 46).

Tens of thousands of whites illegally immigrated into the Choctaw Nation during the late nineteenth century, and by 1890 Choctaws comprised only 25 percent of their own territory's population (Doran, 1975). The tribe passed laws to control immigration and intermarriage, to increase the number of law enforcement and other regulatory personnel, and to heighten the degree of tribal control over the labor of noncitizens (Debo, [1934] 1961; Morrison, 1954; Graebner, 1945). In spite of the initiatives to control non-Indian activities in the area, the high numbers of American citizens in the Choctaw Nation led to continual problems. Even as the Choctaw attempted to exert control over these outsiders, the U.S. government usurped Choctaw control over these citizens and extended the American court system over Indian Territory in the 1880s.

In Mississippi, the Choctaw continued to exist on the margins of the state's cultures. The Choctaw use of the sharecropping system following the Civil War provided the Choctaw the opportunity to "participate as sharecroppers in the economy of the dominant society for the first time without sacrificing their ethnic identity" (Peterson, 1972, p. 1287). The sharecropping system developed as a means of organizing agricultural labor after the Civil War, when slaves no longer worked the land of the larger landowners. Landless people were given access to agricultural land, a shanty, and some degree of support while making a cotton crop. In return the crop was divided in shares, and the white landowner received the largest share. The proportion varied, depending on the amount of goods, agricultural equipment, and animals furnished the sharecropper. Often, the landlord would claim that he was owed more than his tenant's share of the crop, forcing the Choctaw sharecropper permanently in debt to his landlord (Wells, 1982).

Choctaw sharecropping, in spite of its negative economic consequences, made possible the development of stable Choctaw communities patterned more directly after white and black rural communities, but remaining distinctively and exclusively Choctaw. In communities with Indian churches, the majority of children were enrolled in school, usually held in the neighborhood Choctaw church. In spite of slight assistance from the state government for the schools and from local missionary societies to bring Choctaw pastors from Oklahoma, the development depended largely on Choctaw initiative.

Other issues contributed to Choctaw settlement patterns and their "hiding in plain sight." Wolfe (1987) notes that the Choctaw persistently maintained settlement and land use patterns. But for the period 1880–1900,

Choctaw migratory lifeways ended; men stopped silverwork and pottery, and became part of Mississippi's farm labor system.

SUBDIVIDING THE NATION: ALLOTMENT AND THE AFTERMATH

The end of the treaty period in the 1870s ushered in a new perspective on dealing with the "Indian problem." The government, influenced by the views of eastern progressive reformers (such as those espoused in Helen Hunt Jackson's 1881 book, *A Century of Dishonor*) and influential organizations such as the Friends of the Indians, recommended that communal land tenure be replaced by individual land ownership. Cultural assimilation was the goal, and it was expected that the only way to move Indians into the mainstream was to give them the responsibility of land ownership and economic self-sufficiency.

Based on their experiences in Mississippi prior to removal, the Choctaw were opposed to land alienation. An 1839 law proscribed the death penalty for any "Chief, captain, or citizen who should sign a conveyance of Choctaw land" (Debo, [1934] 1961, p. 68). Even though the Treaty of Dancing Rabbit Creek allowed for individual allotments for those who remained in Mississippi, the reality was that such allotments were rarely issued or retained.

The Dawes Act

According to Pauline Strong and Barrik Van Winkle (1993), the Dawes Allotment Act of 1887 was a "major threat to collective ownership of Indian reservation lands through the promotion of individuated identities" (p. 16). The Dawes Act (also called the General Allotment Act or the Dawes Severalty Act) passed Congress on February 8, 1887, under the sponsorship of Senator Henry Dawes of Massachusetts. It was intended to break up reservation lands into individually owned plots as a means to assimilate Native Americans into U.S. society, but also to provide land for numerous settlers clamoring for land.

Senator Dawes, chair of the Senate Indian Committee, believed that the reservation system, whereby tribes held their lands communally, was preventing the economic and cultural development of the Native peoples. The Friends of the Indians, an influential group of philanthropists and reformers in the Northeast, believed that if individual Indians were given plots of land to farm, they would flourish and become integrated into the American economy and culture as middle-class farmers.

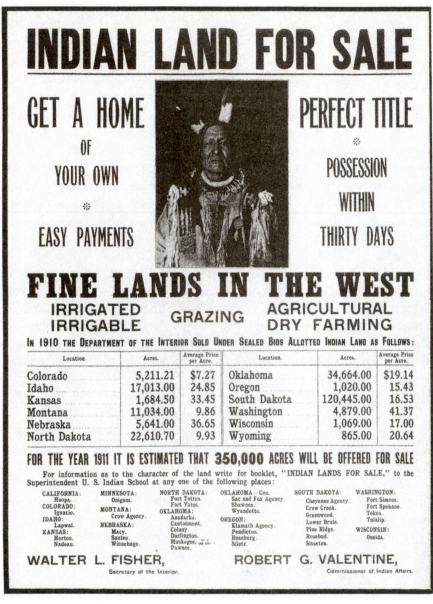

Advertisement by the U.S. Department of the Interior offering surplus lands for sale in 1910–1911. After the government divided communal Indian land for allotment to individual Native Americans under the Dawes Allotment Act of 1887, the surplus land was offered to white settlers, as this advertisement shows. Native Americans lost 90 million acres of land through the allotment policy. (Library of Congress)

The Act had four main provisions. First, it created a series of allotments of various sizes: 160 acres of land to each head of household; 80 acres to each unmarried person over the age of 18 and to each orphan under the age of 18; and 40 acres to each unmarried person under the age of 18. Second, as the land was issued, the government issued a fee patent title on the land, to be held in trust by the federal government for 25 years, during which time the land could not be sold or alienated in any way. Third, the Act allowed people four years to make their own selections of land, after which the government would select the land for them if no individual selection had been made. Fourth, the people who received the allotments ("allottees"), and any other Indians who abandoned their traditional habits of life and who adopted a more civilized life, were conferred the right of citizenship.

One of the first results of the Dawes Act was the massive decrease in Native land base. The indigenous people of America gave up 90 million acres as surplus land between 1887 and 1934, when the Indian Reorganization Act ended allotment. Also, because allottees chose their lands in areas where farming or grazing was to be attempted, the land surrounding the allotments was often provided to non-Indians. As a result, land ownership created a "checkerboard" situation of land ownership, making it difficult for tribal land managers to create effective management programs.

Another legacy of allotment relates to land inheritance. With the complications of land inheritance policies on "trust property," the division of allotments among the many heirs of original allottees is often too difficult to be feasible. Inherited shares are often so small that it can be difficult for heirs to agree how to use allotments.

The impact of the Dawes Act was the final blow to the western lands of the indigenous people. Its lasting impacts can be seen in contemporary society, where tribes face difficulties in managing their tribal lands, developing their economies, and maintaining their communities and cultures.

Dawes Commission

The Dawes Commission was established in 1893 to carry out the policy of allotment. President Grover Cleveland appointed Henry Dawes, Meredith H. Kidd, and Archibald S. McKennon as its original commissioners. In 1895, a reconstituted Dawes Commission was given the authority to survey tribal lands and determine the citizenship status of tribal members.

Initially, the Dawes Act did not apply to the so-called "Five Civilized Tribes" (Cherokee, Chickasaw, Choctaw, Creek, and Seminole). These tribes had already adopted many elements of white European society and culture, which is why they were characterized as "civilized." Moreover, they were protected by treaties that had guaranteed that their tribal lands would remain free of white settlers. However, after these tribes had proven unwilling to voluntarily accept individual allotments of land, the Atoka Agreement of 1897 and the Curtis Act of 1898 amended the Dawes Act to apply to the Five Civilized Tribes. The Curtis Act effectively ended tribal governance by abolishing tribal courts and enforcing allotment. It also stipulated the creation of an authoritative citizenship roll that became known as the Dawes Roll.

In 1904, as the Five Tribes were preparing for allotment, Choctaw Chief McCurtain, along with Cherokee Chief Rogers and other members of the Five Civilized Tribes, proposed the creation of a separate state to span the lands of the Five Civilized Tribes in eastern Oklahoma. The so-called "Sequoyah movement" ended when the admission of the state of Oklahoma became law on June 16, 1906 (Lambert, 2007a).

The Choctaw rolls prepared by the Dawes Commission listed included 19,036 Choctaws "by blood," 1,585 "Intermarried Whites," and 5,994 freedmen (Faiman-Silva, 1997; Lambert, 2007a; McKee, 1971; Wright, 1951). Choctaws "by blood" and intermarried whites were allotted 320 acres, while freedmen were allotted 40 acres. Acreage for about 90 town sites was reserved from allotment, as were over 1.8 million acres of Choctaw and Chickasaw land that was rich in timber, coal, or asphalt (Debo, [1934] 1961). The timber and mineral lands were set aside to be sold at a later date, after which the profits from such sales would be distributed per capita to the nonfreedmen citizens of the Choctaw and Chickasaw tribes (Lambert, 2007a).

In 1902, as part of the Dawes Commission's work in preparing Oklahoma for statehood, the federal government made a second attempt to remove the Choctaw from Mississippi to Oklahoma (Debo, [1940] 1968; Roberts, 1986). Many Choctaws again refused to leave Mississippi. Some, like the group that left from Meridian, Mississippi, for Ardmore, Oklahoma, in 1902, were convinced to move by land speculators who hoped to gain control of their allotments (Levine, 2004). Several communities sold their churches and moved as a group, and the state of Mississippi discontinued the system of Choctaw schools. Some of those later returned "only to find the remaining Choctaw communities scattered and their schools and churches no longer existing" (Peterson, 1987, p. 6).

In Louisiana, the 1880 census offers the first documentation of Choctaw families living at Jena in Catahoula Parish, where 26 people were listed. Linguist Albert Gatschet collected Choctaw phrases from members of these families in 1886. Klopotek notes (2011) that the likely origin of the

Choctaw enumerated on the census shortly after the Civil War is Mississippi, but no direct connections have been made. The 1890 census listed eight families of Choctaws in Catahoula Parish, and two other families in a separate location in the parish.

In addition to the attempts to get the Mississippi Choctaw to move to Oklahoma, the Dawes Commission concluded that some of the Choctaw Indians living in Louisiana were eligible to move to Indian Territory and receive allotments there. With the ratification of a supplemental agreement with the Choctaws and Chickasaws in 1902, the Dawes Commission allowed Catahoula Parish Choctaws to submit testimony toward receiving allotments in Indian Territory as individual Mississippi Choctaws eligible to receive allotments.

Twelve adult Choctaw individuals testified before the Dawes Commission in 1902 (Jena Band in its Federal Acknowledgement Petition, hereafter JBC Petition Historical Report, 1993). The 1902 supplemental agreement gave individuals identified as Mississippi Choctaw six months to settle in the Choctaw nation and one year to provide proof of their settlement in Oklahoma, with March 25, 1903, set as the date for identification as Mississippi Choctaw. Ultimately, the Commission identified 22 individuals from Catahoula Parish as Mississippi Choctaws; however, because of inaction, only 4 were placed on the Final Roll of the Dawes Commission; 18 were identified as Choctaws but not included on the final roll; and 5 were determined to be less than full-blood and not eligible for identification as Mississippi Choctaw (JBC Petition Historical Report, 1993).

Post-Removal Choctaw

The post-Removal Choctaw continued to be a fragmented group of three populations in Oklahoma, Mississippi, and Louisiana. The Dawes Commission tried to reunite the three groups during the allotment process, and some chose to join the Oklahoma Choctaw, but others remained in the home states. Overall, allotment was a major issue among the Choctaw, as the federal government continued its attempt at making farmers out of tribal members. In Oklahoma, the Choctaw tribal government was terminated in 1906 under terms of the Curtis Act; in Mississippi, the Choctaw continued to operate on the edges of society under the sharecropping system, and in Louisiana, there continued to be a small community of Choctaw in Catahoula Parish.

5

❖

Survival, Self-Determination, and Constructing Modern Choctaw Nations

TERMINATION

The Curtis Act of 1898 was meant to do away with the Choctaw Indians of Oklahoma as a separate tribe and to convert its tribal members into American citizen farmers and homemakers. The Act and its companion legislation (the Supplemental Agreement of 1902 and the Five Tribes Act of 1906) created a government that had no real powers (Gibson, 1965). The U.S. government appointed the chief, whose primary duty was to facilitate the settling of the Choctaw-Chickasaw tribal estate as a move toward privatization. In an effort to settle the tribal estate, the federal government sold off some of the tribal timberland between 1913 and 1916, and some of the unallotted mineral lands in 1919 (Lambert, 2007a), and Choctaw individuals received 12 per capita payments by 1925, based on those sales.

In Mississippi, a somewhat opposite plan was in place. John Reeves, a Special Supervisor of the Indian Service, visited the Mississippi Choctaw in 1916 and reported that the land owned was inferior, few owned it, and the Choctaw were "practically destitute, living in decrepit shacks and cabins . . . Tuberculosis and unsanitary conditions generally has caused the death rate to exceed the birth rate" (Strout, 1982, p. 19). In 1917, a committee of the U.S. Congress conducted hearings in Union, Mississippi, and recognized the issues the people were facing. In 1918, an influenza epidemic further decimated the Mississippi Choctaw. Recognizing the failure of removal efforts and the impact of the flu outbreak on the Choctaw, Congress appropriated money in 1918 to establish an agency in Mississippi with the responsibility of working to improve Choctaw health and education (Bounds, 1964; Galloway & Kidwell, 2004).

The establishment of the Choctaw Agency of the Office of Indian Affairs in Philadelphia, Mississippi, in 1918 furthered the development of the separate Choctaw communities that had begun in the 1880s. A land purchase program facilitated a greater concentration of the Choctaw population, as some more isolated sharecroppers were able to move into one of the seven Choctaw communities and begin farming trust land. The population concentration enabled greater numbers of Choctaw children to attend one of the Choctaw schools established in each community. A health program not only brought better medical aid to the Choctaws but also resulted in a separate Choctaw hospital.

CHOCTAW INVOLVEMENT IN WORLD WAR I

With the outbreak of the First World War, Choctaw men were eager to volunteer. American Indian involvement in World War I hinged on the Indian's citizenship. Wise (1931) notes the question related to American Indian citizenship. In determining the citizenship of Indians, the Bureau of Indian Affairs created the rules: An Indian born in the United States was deemed to be a citizen if he, or his father or mother, prior to his birth or before he attained the age of 21 had been allotted land subsequent to May 8, 1906, and had received a patent in fee to his land; or if he were residing in the old Indian Territory on March 3, 1901; or had lived separate and apart from his tribe and had adopted a civilized life (Deloria, 1971 [Wise, 1931]). As a result, it was nearly impossible for the government to accurately determine whether an applicant was a citizen or not.

Men from the Oklahoma National Guard, along with members of the Texas National Guard, were mustered into Camp Bowie, Texas. *The Daily Oklahoman* newspaper (November 4, 1917) noted that the "only purely Indian company in the armies of the United States" was organized in the 142nd infantry company of the 71st Infantry Brigade of the 36th Division at Camp Bowie, near Fort Worth, Texas. Formed in July 1917, just a few months after the United States entered World War I, the 36th Infantry Division first saw combat in France in 1918. The insignia of the 36th Infantry Division, the "Texas" division, represented the division's members of the National Guard units from Texas and Oklahoma during World War I.

The "T" in the division's insignia represented Texas; and the arrowhead, Oklahoma. The division was also sometimes called the "Lone Star" division, again symbolizing its Texas roots.

Some of the history of the 36th Division details the experiences of the Choctaw and other Indians from Oklahoma. The soldiers saw a great deal of action during the Meuse-Argonne offensive and helped break through the German lines during the Forest Farm operation at the Aisne River (White, 1979).

The greatest contribution of the 36th, however, was in communications. Suspecting that the Germans were intercepting messages, Colonel Alfred W. Bloor of Austin, the Commanding Officer of the 142nd Infantry, detailed an idea in a report to General Smith, dated January 23, 1919. In the report, Bloor assigned Indians to the company telephones to transmit information, noting, "We were confident that the possibilities of the telephone had been obtained without its hazards" (Deloria, in Wise, 1971, p. 328).

Two famous Choctaw warriors of World War I were Otis W. Leader and Joseph Oklahombi. Leader, sometimes identified as Chickasaw, was selected to pose as the model representative of the newly arrived American soldiers by a French artist commissioned to paint portraits of the Allied army by the French government (Foreman, 1943). His portrait and statue are in Paris and London. Leader won the French Croix de Guerre twice, a Purple Heart, and nine Battle Stars. Leader

Joseph Oklahombi, Choctaw Code Talker during World War I. Oklahombi, whose name means "people killer" in the Choctaw language, was considered "Oklahoma's Greatest Hero." He was awarded the Silver Star with the Victory Ribbon from the United States, and from Marshal Henri-Philippe Pétain he received the Croix de Guerre, one of France's highest military honors. (Oklahoma Historical Society/Getty Images)

was called one of the "war's greatest fighting machines" by General Pershing (Scribner, n.d.).

The exploits of Joseph Oklahombi were summed up in a "Briefly Told" column in the *Dearborn Independent* (November 5, 1921, p. 16). The article describing Oklahombi opened:

> Capturing 171 German prisoners single-handed, Joseph Oklahombi, a Choctaw Indian, was decorated and cited by Marshall Pétain, of France, as the second greatest hero that the war produced. Alvin York ranks first. Oklahombi, which in Choctaw means "man-killer" lives in obscurity on a small farm near Idabel, Oklahoma. The citation reads (in part):
>
> > Under a violent barrage, he dashed to the attack of the enemy position, covering 200 yards through barbed wire entanglements. He rushed on machine gun nests, capturing 171 prisoners. He stormed a strongly held position containing a number of trench mortars, turned the captured guns on the enemy and held said position for four days, in spite of a constant barrage of large projectiles and gas shells. He crossed No Man's Land many times to get information concerning his wounded comrades.

Foreman (1943) also documents Oklahombi's exploits.

At the end of the war, the surviving Choctaw soldiers returned to a rapidly changing lifestyle. Congress granted citizenship to honorably discharged Indian veterans in 1919, under terms of the Act of November 6, 1919, 41 Stat. L. 350); five years later, all Indians were granted citizenship under the Act of June 2, 1924, 43 Stat. L. 253 (Barsh, 1991).

AFTER THE WAR

In 1921, the Choctaw Agency in Mississippi began a program of "colonization" aimed at creating Mississippi Choctaw "colonies"—small plots of land from 20 to 40 acres in seven major areas—that would be resold to full-blood Choctaws through a loan program (Strout, 1982). In this manner, it was hoped that the Choctaws would be able to grow enough of their own food for subsistence and, by locating schools on some of the land, strengthen the Choctaw educational system that was lost as a result of the Dawes commission removal attempts (Brescia, 1982; Peterson, 1992).

In some ways, the plan was successful; in other ways, not so. Within 10 years, nearly 10,000 acres of land had been bought by the Choctaw

---

CHOCTAW CODE TALKERS

An American officer, Colonel A. W. Bloor, noticed a number of American Indians serving with him in the 142nd Infantry in France. Overhearing two Choctaw Indians speaking with each other, he realized he could not understand them. With the active cooperation of his Choctaw soldiers, he tested and deployed a code, using the Choctaw language in place of regular military code.

Nineteen Choctaw men have been documented as being the first to use their own language as a "code" to transmit military messages. During World War I, German forces tapped into the U.S. Army's phone lines and were able to learn the location of Allied Forces and their supply depots. When the Choctaw men were put on the phones and talked in their Native speech, the Germans couldn't effectively spy on the transmissions.

On November 15, 2008, The Code Talkers Recognition Act of 2008 (Public Law 110–420), was signed into law by President George W. Bush, which recognizes every Native American code talker who served in the U.S. military during World War I or World War II, with the exception of the already-awarded Navajo, with a Congressional Gold Medal for his tribe, to be retained by the Smithsonian Institution, and a silver medal duplicate to each code talker.

World War I Choctaw code talkers were Albert Billy, Mitchell Bobb, Victor Brown, Ben Carterby, Ben Colbert, George Davenport, Joe Davenport, James Edwards, Tobias Frazier, Ben Hampton, Noel Johnson, Otis Leader, Solomon Louis, Pete Maytubby, Jeff Nelson, Joseph Oklahombi, Robert Taylor, Walter Veach, and Calvin Wilson. World War II Choctaw Code Talkers included Schlicht Billy, Andrew Perry, Davis Pickens, and Forreston T. Baker.

Agency and resold to the Choctaw farmers; seven schools had been constructed and were operating (Strout, 1982). However, the plots of land were too small and too poor to actually support the families, let alone provide enough income to allow the farmers to pay off the loans. Thus, most of the loans were defaulted on, creating a reservation of sorts composed of these so-called "reimbursable lands" (Peterson, 1992, p. 142).

In Oklahoma, the Choctaw and Chickasaw held in common "nearly 400,000 acres containing about two billion tons of coal and asphalt" (Lambert, 2007a, p. 52) by 1938. In the late 1940s, the U.S. government made an offer of $3.5 million for this land, but that amount was revised upward to as much as $8.5 million as a result of testimony provided by Choctaw Chief Harry J. W. Belvin (Hunke, 1986). The Choctaw and Chickasaw voted to accept the terms of the sale and received a per capita payment at mid-century (Wright, 1951).

THE INDIAN "NEW DEAL" AND REORGANIZATION

The federal government's policy of allotment was reversed under three pieces of legislation that formed collectively what has been termed "The Indian New Deal." The Indian Reorganization Act of 1934 (IRA) was aimed at decreasing federal control of American Indian affairs and increasing Indian self-government and responsibility. The Johnson-O'Malley Act of 1934 was aimed at improving Indian education by authorizing financial support for educational, medical, agricultural, and social welfare services to lessen the impact of racism and discrimination on Indian children. The Indian Arts and Crafts Board Act of 1935 promoted economic self-sufficiency of reservations by improving the quality of Native arts and crafts and expanding their distribution (Watkins, 2018).

The IRA had the most far-reaching effects of the three bills. It ended the allotment of Native American land through nullification of the 1887 Dawes Act. It also restored any surplus reservation lands that the Dawes Act had created, and called for reorganization of tribal governments under either a constitutional model or charters giving Indians the power to manage their internal affairs. About 160 tribes or villages adopted written constitutions under the IRA's provisions.

A tribal convention in 1934 endorsed the IRA, but that legislation excluded Oklahoma tribes. In 1936, the federal government passed the Oklahoma Indian Welfare Act to bring Oklahoma Indians under the same program as those under the IRA. The Choctaw Nation refused to recognize the Oklahoma Indian Welfare Act of 1936 and continued to operate under its traditional government, using an advisory council (Clark, 2009). As Lambert (2007a) notes, none of the Five Civilized Tribes—including the Choctaw—chose to "reorganize" (p. 56). Tribal support of the IRA among other tribes varied as well; some tribes were concerned that the legislation cemented nontraditional ways of governing members, whereas others were supportive of the economic development it promoted. Although the IRA did not concern itself with the issue of Native American treaties, it did allow the revival and perpetuation of the concept of tribal sovereignty. A sense of tribal consciousness was emphasized by the policies, but the reform showed little concern or awareness of the complexity of tribal relations and tensions.

In Mississippi, the IRA put the Mississippi Choctaw on an opposite trajectory. The Act provided the authority of the Choctaw Agency to purchase more land for the benefit of the Choctaw people, and almost 18,000 acres were held in trust for the Choctaw by the agency. The IRA created an opportunity for the Mississippi Indians to once again enter the mainstream of American Indian politics, and Choctaw Agency Superintendent Hector appointed Choctaw members to the Choctaw Tribal Business Committee to consider the Act. The Committee, comprised of 17 representatives from the seven communities—three each from the communities of Conehatta, Tucker, and Pearl River; and two from the smaller districts of Red Water, Standing Pine, Bogue Chitto, and Bogue Homa—was almost completely under the control of the Choctaw Agency superintendent and met only when called together by the superintendent (Osburn, 2007). A rival organization, the Mississippi Choctaw Indian Federation, formed shortly after (Strout, 1982).

Through 1934 and into 1935, the two organizations seemed to be at odds, although each indicated it was working toward tribal governance. Superintendent Hector was opposed to the Federation, writing, "The organization tried to make trouble and succeeded to some degree" (Strout, 1982, p. 27). The Business Committee, however, was merely an exercise in representative government and had no powers to deal with any issues of importance to tribal members.

When Joe Jennings, a special agent for the Office of Indian Affairs, traveled to Mississippi in June 1936 to establish the official IRA government, the two organizations were both still operating. Shortly thereafter, Jennings determined the Mississippi Choctaw were not eligible to use the IRA because they were not a tribe and did not live on trust lands (Osburn, 2007).

Ultimately, perhaps driven by the Shell Oil Company interest in oil leases on Choctaw lands in the Pearl River district in 1944, the reimbursable lands were reclassified as a reservation in 1944, and the Choctaws were declared a tribe by the secretary of the interior. On April 20, 1945, the Choctaws approved the constitution and a 16-member tribal council, but the tribal council still had little power or influence over tribal affairs. Still, once the tribal constitution was accepted by the federal government, the Mississippi Band of Choctaw Indians (MBCI) received federal recognition as a tribe once more, ending more than 100 years without a governing structure. Their recognition reestablished a direct relationship with the federal government and moved them out from under the jurisdiction of the state of Mississippi.

Following recognition by the United States as an American Indian tribe, the MBCI slowly expanded its governance structures. Much of the initial work of the tribe was done under the strictures of the Choctaw Agency of the Bureau of Indian Affairs (BIA), and meetings usually were held at the behest of the Agency superintendent. The government of the fledgling Mississippi Band of Choctaw Indians moved forward, but still primarily under the control of the BIA. In July of 1945, the first regular meeting of the Choctaw Tribal Council was held, and Joe Chitto of the Standing Pine Community was selected as chairman of the tribal council; Emmett York took over as chairman in 1949, before Phillip Martin took over as tribal chairman in 1959 (Gantt, 2013). Phillip Martin was reelected to the tribal council and served as tribal chairman from 1959 to 1966, and then again from 1971 to 1975, the position only becoming a full-time paid job in 1962.

Numerous authors have described the struggle that occurred between the administrative management of the tribal concerns by the Bureau of Indian Affairs and the desires of the Tribal Council of the Mississippi Band (Gantt, 2013; McKee & Murray, 1986; Peterson, 1992; Strout, 1982). The BIA continued to be a powerful force in the affairs of the Mississippi Band of Choctaw, as termination and relocation were major policies of the federal government during this time (McKee & Murray, 1986; Peterson, 1992). Still, however, the Tribe continued on the twin roads of economic development and self-governance, on parallel and intertwining tracks.

It was also at about this time that the community in Louisiana began getting noticed. The Choctaw Indian community in the vicinity of Jena became known to outsiders mostly because of the actions by Mattie Penick to create educational opportunities for the Choctaw children in the Jena area during 1930s. The Penick School operated between 1932 and 1938 in several buildings in several locations, as a means of educating the Choctaw, who weren't allowed to attend public school but refused to attend schools for African American students in the deeply segregated state (JBC Summary, 1993; Klopotek, 2011).

The education concerns also offered another opportunity for the Jena Band to become recognized as "Mississippi Choctaw." As early as 1934, the Choctaw Agency Superintendent A. C. Hector proposed that the Jena Band be relocated to Mississippi when land there could be purchased for them. In 1937, it was suggested that the families at Jena should be offered land at Pearl River, Mississippi, so that their children could attend school there rather than in the Jena area. In 1938, Assistant Commissioner of Indian Affairs William Zimmerman suggested that the Jena Band be removed to Mississippi, but no action was taken due to the unavailability of homes in the area (JBC Summary, 1993).

Although there was no formal governance structure in place among these families, the White Rock Indian Cemetery, located across Trout Creek from Eden, Louisiana, served as a community locus in many ways. Tribal members took advantage of regular monthly gatherings to clean the cemetery, discuss community issues, and reach consensus on topics of importance (JBC Summary, 1993).

CHOCTAWS IN WORLD WAR II

World War II saw many members of the Choctaw tribes in Oklahoma and Mississippi enlist. However, it's difficult to determine just how many of the Mississippi Choctaw participated in the armed services because the Mississippi Band of Choctaw Indians didn't obtain formal recognition until 1945. However, one such individual with Choctaw heritage was Van T. Barfoot. Barfoot was born in Edinburg, Mississippi, in 1919. His grandmother was Choctaw, but because his parents never enrolled him, Barfoot was not an official member of the Choctaw Nation of Oklahoma; and because the Mississippi Band of Choctaw Indians didn't get reorganized until 1945, he was not officially a member of the Mississippi Band of Choctaw Indians.

Barfoot's actions in the World War II, however, earned him military honors. In December 1941, Barfoot served with the 1st Infantry Division in Louisiana and Puerto Rico, and was promoted to sergeant and sent to the Headquarters Amphibious Force Atlantic Fleet in Quantico, Virginia. There, Barfoot served until 1943, when the unit was deactivated. In late January 1944, he was sent to Anzio, Italy, where he joined the 157th Infantry Regiment, 45th Infantry Division. Barfoot scouted and patrolled the German lines.

On the morning of May 23, 1944, the company was ordered to attack. Barfoot, who knew the terrain and minefield situated in front of the German position, asked for permission to lead a squad. Launching a hand grenade, Barfoot was successful in taking out a German machine gun nest and crew. Upon entering the German trench, Barfoot killed two soldiers and captured three others. As the entire crew surrendered to Barfoot, he captured 17 German soldiers and killed 8.

Later that day, with three Tiger tanks, the Germans launched a counterattack. With a bazooka, Barfoot disabled the lead tank, killing part of the German crew with a Thompson submachine gun. Advancing into the enemy-held territory, Barfoot destroyed an abandoned German artillery piece and helped two wounded soldiers from his squad upon his return.

Subsequent to the action, and before his award, Barfoot was promoted to Second Lieutenant. According to the U.S. Army Center of Military History, Barfoot's citation reads:

> For conspicuous gallantry and intrepidity at the risk of life above and beyond the call of duty on 23 May 1944, near Carano, Italy. With his platoon heavily engaged during an assault against forces well entrenched on commanding ground, 2d Lt. Barfoot (then Tech. Sgt.) moved off alone upon the enemy left flank. He crawled to the proximity of one

machinegun nest and made a direct hit on it with a hand grenade, killing two and wounding three Germans. He continued along the German defense line to another machinegun emplacement, and with his tommygun killed two and captured three soldiers. Members of another enemy machinegun crew then abandoned their position and gave themselves up to Sgt. Barfoot. Leaving the prisoners for his support squad to pick up, he proceeded to mop up positions in the immediate area, capturing more prisoners and bringing his total count to 17. Later that day, after he had reorganized his men and consolidated the newly captured ground, the enemy launched a fierce armored counterattack directly at his platoon positions. Securing a bazooka, Sgt. Barfoot took up an exposed position directly in front of three advancing Mark VI tanks. From a distance of 75 yards his first shot destroyed the track of the leading tank, effectively disabling it, while the other two changed direction toward the flank. As the crew of the disabled tank dismounted, Sgt. Barfoot killed three of them with his tommygun. He continued onward into enemy terrain and destroyed a recently abandoned German fieldpiece with a demolition charge placed in the breech. While returning to his platoon position, Sgt. Barfoot, though greatly fatigued by his Herculean efforts, assisted two of his seriously wounded men 1,700 yards to a position of safety. Sgt. Barfoot's extraordinary heroism, demonstration of magnificent valor, and aggressive determination in the face of pointblank fire are a perpetual inspiration to his fellow soldiers. ("Barfoot, Van T.," 2008)

AFTER WORLD WAR II

In Oklahoma, things continued along the path to assimilation. In the late 1940s, anthropologist Alexander Spoehr concluded that, due in part to the Oklahoma Choctaw pursuit of social and cultural assimilation, Choctaw kinship in Oklahoma had "lost its importance as a means of widely establishing and regulating social relations" and "of integrating the local group" (1947, p. 208). Angie Debo and Muriel Wright, widely known as two of the most respected scholars on Choctaw history, believed the Choctaw to be on the verge of extinction as autonomous organizations (Lambert, 2007a).

By 1946, federal philosophies concerning American Indians had changed, and the Bureau of Indian Affairs' main objective was to organize the tribes so that they could manage their own affairs and adapt their native institutions and culture to modern society. This policy—called "termination"—led to the view that Indian schools, clinics, and hospitals (as well as tribal governments) were unnecessary. It was felt that the BIA should be abolished, and federal supervision and control over the Indian should be terminated.

In 1948, Harry J. W. Belvin was appointed by the president as the seventh Choctaw chief of the twentieth century. Chief Belvin lived up to the government's desires by attempting to sell and distribute the proceeds from the sale of the remaining Choctaw tribal lands to Choctaw individuals. Kotlowski (2002) describes Belvin as an assimilationist and a "wily opportunist," noting that Belvin successfully lobbied the Interior Department to hold a tribal election (p. 22). President Truman named him chief after he was elected on June 21, 1948. He was twice reelected, and then he stopped requesting elections, which ceased after 1954. It was during Belvin's tenure, on August 1, 1953, that Congress passed the Termination Act (House Concurrent Resolution 108). The intention of the Act was to free Indians from federal supervision, abolish the BIA, and allow Native Americans to become "full-fledged" American citizens.

As part of the termination policy, programs established procedures whereby tribal members could obtain training. Some of these programs were tied to the Indian Relocation Act of 1956 (also known as the Adult Vocational Training Program). Tribal adults from reservations were encouraged to leave the reservation and relocate to urban areas such as Chicago, Dallas, Denver, Minneapolis-St. Paul, San Francisco, and others. As Strout (1982) pointed out, mostly the program failed. There were no special programs to help the transplanted individuals adjust to city life, and without familiar family and social structures, many of those who participated moved from rural poverty to urban poverty.

However, in spite of the federal government's desires to improve the lifestyle of American Indians, little changed among the Mississippi Band of Choctaw Indians. A statement by MBCI Chairman Phillip Martin, at the American Indian Chicago Conference in 1961, illustrated the rural poverty levels of the tribal members:

> The income of an average family is approximately $600.00 yearly while only a few enjoy a yearly income of approximately $2,000.00. . . . Only a few Choctaw are skilled workers. A few are heavy-road equipment operators. Most Choctaws are farm laborers. The average wage for a farm-laborer is approximately $2.50 a day which is ordinarily from sun-up to sun-down or twelve hours. . . . Farming, stock raising, poultry, pulpwood and lumber industries are the only source of income (as quoted in McKee & Murray, 1986, p. 126)

In Oklahoma, Belvin and U.S. Representative Carl Albert secured legislation to terminate the Choctaw tribe. HR 2722 provided for the sale of more than 16,000 acres of Choctaw land, with the proceeds to be divided on a per capita basis. The bill passed both houses of Congress during the summer of 1959. It created a three-year window for the tribe to act, setting 1962 as the year when federal supervision of the tribe would cease.

However, because of the tribe's inability to obtain a full accounting of its property, and facing lawsuits from parties who were claiming title to its lands, the tribe requested a three-year extension, not repeal, of the act. It wasn't until 1962, however, that the BIA agreed to an extension (Kotlowski, 2002). In 1968, after other previous extensions, Congress postponed the date of termination again, until August 25, 1970.

Accordingly, in 1970, Congress allowed members of the Five Civilized Tribes to elect their own chiefs (Lambert, 2007a). Belvin won reelection in 1971 through "dirty politics" (Kotlowski, 2002). However, David Gardner, who advocated for industrial development and educational opportunities, as well as for democratic practices for the Choctaw Nation, was elected in 1975, breaking the hold of the assimilationist Belvin.

While the Oklahoma Choctaw were moving purposefully toward Termination, the Mississippi Band of Choctaw Indians (MBCI) moved toward development. McKee and Murray (1986) note the impact of various federal programs on the Mississippi Band of Choctaws. The Area Development Act of 1961 and its successor, the Economic Development Administration Act of 1965, made it possible for Indian reservations to receive benefits; the 1962 Manpower Development and Training Act provided benefits to American Indians; and the Economic Opportunity Act of 1964 allowed Indian communities to become sponsoring agencies for such programs as Head Start and Upward Bound.

The MBCI actively got involved with economic development shortly thereafter. In 1963, the MBCI purchased a portion of the D.L. Fair Lumber Company property at Louisville, Mississippi, and established the Louisville Cabinet Company. The company was intended to provide employment opportunities for Choctaw tribal members, but because of the commuting distance of 20 miles, coupled with the fact that few tribal members had reliable transportation, not many Choctaw individuals were able to find employment opportunities there (McKee & Murray, 1986).

Peterson (1992) notes that 1964 can be marked as a turning point for the MBCI, with the establishment of the Choctaw Central High School and the passage of the Civil Rights Act. In 1964, the council authorized the chairman and secretary-treasurer to execute a lease of the Louisville site with Winston Industries, then later to Spartus Corporation. This business deal allowed the tribe to pay off the original loan, and lasted into the late 1970s (McKee & Murray, 1986).

A $15,000 planning grant in 1964 led to the establishment of a Community Action Agency, and in less than 20 years the MBCI was administering over $10 million in federal grants and contracts (Peterson, 1992). Martin resigned as tribal chairman to take over the Community Action Agency, and Emmett York became chairman. The Choctaw Community Action Program developed social assistance programs such as early childhood education (Head Start and related programs), community health initiatives, emergency food distribution, and other social services. Advisory councils for some of these programs offered opportunities for more Choctaw people to have an active voice in the operation of programs on the reservation.

The 1968 passage of the Indian Civil Rights Act formally ended the policy of termination. The Act created new goals aimed at raising the standard of living of the Indian, providing individuals with the option of remaining on a reservation or moving to a city, and increasing the Indian's opportunity to share in the benefits of modern America (McKee & Murray, 1986). In June 1970, Congress repealed the termination act. In July 1970, President Nixon's message of "self-determination without termination" resonated with American Indians. In conjunction with the Alaska Native Claims Settlement Act of 1971, and the Indian Self-Determination and Education Assistance Act of 1975, tribal governance received support from the U.S. government, rather than a push for dissolution.

SELF-DETERMINATION AND ECONOMIC DEVELOPMENT

In Oklahoma, David Gardner's election in 1975 created opportunities for the Choctaw Nation of Oklahoma to expand its limited political views as a nation. Gardner was able to acquire the former campus of the Presbyterian College in Durant for a new headquarters for the tribal government in 1976. However, in 1978, Gardner developed cancer, specifically lymphoma; only two and a half years into his four-year term, he died, leaving his family, staff, and the Choctaw people stunned and devastated.

Gardner's assistant chief, Hollis Roberts, was the next elected chief. A key event in Robert's administration was the passage of a new constitution in 1983, the first since 1860. As a result of a 1981 court case that argued the 1860 constitution was still valid and binding, the secretary of the interior held an election consisting of a referendum and also a determination of who would be eligible for tribal membership. Membership was specified to be based on the Dawes Rolls, and the tribal members decided that a tribal member must be able to trace direct relationship with at least one person on the Dawes Rolls; they also allowed women to vote and created a new tripartite government structure (Lambert, 2007a).

The new government established by the 1983 constitution consisted of the executive department headed by the chief, a legislative branch comprised of a tribal council, and a three-member tribal court as the judicial department. In the second stage of the referendum, Choctaws voted on whether to adopt a new constitution incorporating the results of the first referendum. In the third stage, a new chief and tribal council were elected.

After the passage of the 1983 constitution, tribal leaders strengthened and actively promoted the development of ties between Choctaw individuals and the tribal government. A tribal newspaper, *Bishinik* (now *Biskinik*), was established to provide Choctaws with news about tribal matters and about Choctaw births, deaths, and birthdays. The construction of additional tribal community centers, a high priority of tribal leaders in the early 1980s, also strengthened ties among Choctaws and ties between Choctaws and the tribal government.

Using the Indian Self-Determination and Education Assistance Act (ISDEAA) of 1975, the Choctaw Nation took over programs that had previously been administered and provided by the BIA and the Indian Health Service (IHS). Vocational training, food distribution, and early childhood development programs flourished under Roberts and his Assistant Chief Gregory Pyle. In 1965, the Tribe took over management of the IHS hospital in Talihina, as well as IHS clinics in Hugo, Broken Bow, and McAlester. By 1991, the tribe was administering 21 million dollars of federal program funding.

Tribal economic growth continued, in spite of issues of tribal governance. In June 1997, a federal court found Chief Roberts guilty of sexually abusing female tribal employees and sentenced him to 11 years in jail. With Roberts' imprisonment, Assistant Chief Pyle assumed the role of chief.

Pyle continued tribal focus on health care issues, but also expanded tribal business enterprises, so much so that the value of the tribe's assets has increased from $14.5 million in 1981 to $144 million in 2002 (Lambert, 2007a). With his resignation in April of 2014, Assistant Chief Gary Batton moved into the leadership position, appointing Jack Austin Jr. as his assistant chief.

In Mississippi, the early 1970s saw the MBCI government developing further through consolidation of programs and economic opportunity. As a result of the need for administrative control of the various programs on the reservation, a revised constitution and bylaws was proposed by the tribal council, ratified by majority vote of the tribe, and put into effect in 1975. The new constitution more clearly separated the government into executive and legislative branches, and provided for the direct election of the tribal chief by the general Choctaw membership rather than by appointment by the tribal council every two years.

The new structure established the chief as the principal executive officer of the tribe and as head of the executive branch of tribal government, with the power to negotiate contracts, to administer the operation of tribal government, to prepare budgets and financial reports, and to preside over the meetings of Council. The chief's term was expanded to four years from the previous two-year term, with no term limits imposed.

The establishment of the office of chief strengthened the executive function of tribal government. It was also an act of self-determination as the office of chief had been abolished and prohibited under state law in the 1830s. Actions by the chief, however, still required approval from the Council. The first elected chief in 1975 was Calvin Isaac. In 1979, Phillip Martin was elected chief of the MBCI, a position he held until 2007, when Beasley Denson was elected the third chief of the tribe since the adoption of the modern constitution.

The Mississippi Band of Choctaw Indians continued their economic development into the 1970s, with expansion of the Choctaw Industrial Park in 1978. As noted earlier, self-determination and economic development were so closely intertwined that it has been difficult to separate the two. In 1979, the MBCI entered into agreements with the Packard

Choctaw chief Phillip Martin in 2004. He was first elected chief in 1979, and held the position until 2007. Martin's vision and drive helped make the Mississippi Band of Choctaw Indians the thriving cultural and economic force it is today. (National Aeronautics and Space Administration)

Electric Division of General Motors to produce wire harness assemblies for Chevrolet pickup trucks and Buick La Sabres. The Tribe reached an agreement with the American Greetings Corporation to hand-finish quality greeting cards in 1981 (Brescia, 1982; McKee & Murray, 1986).

Chahta Enterprises, which had been the primary office of the Tribe overseeing development, opened its second plant in 1983; Choctaw Electronics Enterprise opened in 1985 to manufacture automobile radio speakers. In 1986, Chahta Enterprises opened its third plant in DeKalb, Mississippi, to assemble automotive and nonautomotive wiring harnesses. Later that same year, Choctaw Manufacturing Enterprise, created to produce a variety of electronic devices and circuit boards for automotive and other industries, opened in the Leake County Industrial Park. Throughout this time until present, numerous other Tribal enterprises have been developed, and the Tribe is seen as a major economic force in central Mississippi.

In Louisiana, the biggest event in the formalization of the Jena Band began in 1974, with the formalization of articles of incorporation for the "Jena Band of Choctaw Indians of Louisiana." Its purpose was to promote and preserve the cultural heritage of the Choctaw peoples and to administer government grants and private donations. The articles established a five-member tribal council with three-year terms. They also required an annual meeting of the corporation's membership. Later that year, the state legislature passed a resolution that formally recognized "the Choctaw Indian community at Jena, Louisiana, as an Indian tribe" (Gregory, 1977, p. 14).

Leaders of the corporation varied over time, but many of them were members of the Jackson, Lewis, and Allen families. Although the early portion of the corporation's time was spent on economic issues, from 1979 to 1995, the Tribe became focused on gaining federal recognition as an Indian Tribe under the Office of Federal Acknowledgment in addition to providing services for tribal members (Klopeotek, 2011).

Subsequently, the new corporation of Jena Indians received funds from the office of Housing and Urban Development as well as separate grants to provide research funds to support the Jena Band's efforts to gain federal recognition. Grants from the Administration for Native Americans in 1984 and 1988 were also applied to recognition pursuits.

Ultimately, tribal recognition under the Office of Federal Acknowledgment (OFA) procedures, under which the Jena made their application, required three main components: a detailed genealogy to prove that it was descended from people identified in the historic record as "Indians"; a history that demonstrated that the tribe had existed as an Indian community throughout time covered by available historical records; and an anthropological report that documented present community relations, culture, and social and political structures (Klopotek, 2011).

The first attempt at recognition was withdrawn because of deficiencies identified by the OFA. The Jena initially tried to create documentation between the contemporary group and some of the named individuals identified in the very early census records. The group was able to get the Mississippi Band of Choctaw to assert that the Jena Band's ancestors were "Mississippi Choctaw," thereby releasing the group from having to prove their connection to those initial founding families. Another attempt to gain recognition by an act of Congress also met with failure when President Bush withheld approval of Senate 3095. According to the memorandum dated October 21, 1992, the bill's use of the term *restore* was in error, as the Jena had never been recognized as an Indian tribe, but rather as individual Indians, and therefore not subject to a legislative remedy of "restoration."

In spite of these false starts, the Jena continued to push forward. Proceeding from this, the Jena started another petition, utilizing historians and anthropologists to gather the necessary materials to create the documents required by the OFA. The group's petition was approved by BIA Director Ada Deer on September 27, 1994, and the Jena Tribe gained federal recognition as an Indian tribe in 1995.

GAMING

On October 17, 1988, the 100th Congress enacted the Indian Gaming Regulatory Act (IGRA) as Public Law 100-497. The Act allows Indian tribal governments to open Class III casinos in states where state policy allows gaming. It also provides an administrative process for regulating gaming on Indian lands. Gaming is seen as a means of "promoting tribal economic development, self-sufficiency, and strong tribal governments."

Under the terms of the Act, the Choctaw Nation and the state of Oklahoma had to a reach an agreement (a "compact") that outlined how the gaming facilities would be regulated. The compacts involve the tribe, the state, and the federal government. Because the casinos are not taxed, revenues flow to the tribe as tax-equivalent funds to provide services to tribal members.

The Choctaw began their gaming operations in 1988 with the construction of a high-stakes bingo palace in Durant, Oklahoma. Roberts added three other bingo palaces and expanded advertising to reach more customers. Chief Pyle added other "casinos" and proved instrumental in changing the gaming landscape in Oklahoma through his leadership in the passage of Oklahoma State Question 712, which enacted the Oklahoma State Tribal

INDIAN GAMING REGULATORY ACT

The Indian Gaming Regulatory Act established the National Indian Gaming Commission and gave it a regulatory mandate. The law also delegated new authority to the U.S. Department of the Interior and created new federal offenses, giving the U.S. Department of Justice authority to prosecute them.

The Act established three classes of games, with a different regulatory scheme for each:

The IGRA defines Class I gaming as "social games solely for prizes of minimal value or traditional forms of Indian gaming engaged in by individuals as a part of, or in connection with, tribal ceremonies or celebrations" [25 CFR §2703(6)]. These sorts of games might be based on traditional practices such as ceremonial footraces or traditional games of chance such as the moccasin game, where an object is hidden within one of several moccasins, and the opposing player attempts to guess which moccasin holds the hidden object. The Act goes on further to note that these sorts of games are not regulated under the Act.

Class II is defined as "the game of chance commonly known as bingo (whether or not electronic, computer, or other technologic aids are used in connection therewith)" [25 CFR §2703(7)]. It also includes "pull-tabs, lotto, punch boards, tip jars, instant bingo, and other games similar to bingo" if played in the same location, as well as card games that are explicitly authorized or not explicitly prohibited by the State where the casino is located. It excludes any banking card games (where the player competes against "the house"), including baccarat, *chemin de fer*, or blackjack ("21"). It also excludes electronic or electromechanical facsimiles of any game of chance or slot machines of any kind. The Tribe is responsible for regulating gaming with oversight by the Indian Gaming Regulatory Commission.

Class III gaming is extremely broad, but is defined as "all forms of gaming that are not class I gaming or class II gaming" [25 CFR §2703(8)]. These sorts of games include games commonly played at casinos such as slot machines, blackjack, craps, and roulette. Other wagering games and electronic facsimiles of other games of chance also fall into the class III category. The IGRA requires the tribe and the state where the casino is located to enter into a "Compact" [25 CFR §2710(d)] governing the conduct of gaming activities.

The regulatory scheme for class III gaming is more complex than a casual reading of the statute might suggest. Although Congress clearly intended regulatory issues to be addressed in Tribal–State compacts, it left a number of key functions in federal hands, including approval authority over compacts, management contracts, and Tribal gaming ordinances. Congress also vested the Commission with broad authority to issue regulations in furtherance of the purposes of the Act. Accordingly, the Commission plays a key role in the regulation of class II and III gaming.

Gaming Act (OSTGA) of 2004. As a result of the act, 24 other tribes had entered into tribal "compacts" with the state by the following year.

After gaming, the most visible Choctaw tribal businesses are travel plazas. Most of the tribe's travel plazas, spread across southeastern Oklahoma, offer gasoline, convenience stores, small restaurants, spaces for pull-tab gaming, and discount cigarettes. Roberts built travel plazas in more than a half-dozen Choctaw Nation communities, and Pyle expanded this important source of tribal income and jobs throughout his tenure. In addition, the Nation invested in manufacturing and other commercial enterprises.

Much like the Oklahoma Choctaw economy, the Mississippi Band of Choctaw Indians derive the majority of their tribal income through their gaming and entertainment facilities. Much of the same processes operate in Mississippi as they do in Oklahoma, with tribal and state compacts in place and regulated under the IGRA.

The MBCI opened the Silver Star Hotel and Casino in 1994, the Golden Moon Hotel in 2002, and the Bok Homa Casino in 2010. The Silver Star Hotel and Casino, the Golden Moon Hotel and The Arena concert venue, Geyser Falls Water Theme Park, Clear Water Key and Beach Club, and the 36-hole Dancing Rabbit Golf Club are part of the Pearl River Resort at Choctaw, Mississippi. The income generated by these gaming and entertainment facilities (part of the $400 million revenues in FY 2010) has helped the MBCI invest in new school construction, new early childhood development, academic scholarships, and other programs. Additional aspects of the MBCI economic enterprises are available in its Tribal Profile (MBCI, 2012).

The MBCI website (http://www.choctaw.org) notes that the Tribe is one of Mississippi's top five largest private employers and that it has created about 5,750 jobs since 1969. McKee and Murray (1986) provide some figures relating to the changes in Choctaw income: in 1970, family median income for Choctaw was $3,120, compared with $6,068 for Mississippi and $9,590 for the nation. In 1980, family median income for Choctaw increased to $8,676, Mississippi income to $14,603, and the national average to $19,908. Although the Choctaw figures were still far below Mississippi and national averages, they had risen percentage-wise in relation to the others. Currently, income and benefits (in 2016 inflation-adjusted dollars) based on the American Community Survey (ACS) estimates place the Mississippi Band of Choctaw Indians median household income at $35,732 and mean household income at $41,686 for the Mississippi Choctaw Reservation and Off-Reservation Trust Land (U.S. Census Bureau, 2018a). Statewide, the median household income was $40,528 (U.S. Census Bureau, 2018b).

Economic development is closely tied to gaming for the Jena Band. The Choctaw Pines Casino is located in Dry Prong, Louisiana, approximately 25 miles southwest of Jena. The casino opened in 2013, and provides funding for tribal educational and housing programs. In 2017, the tribe announced plans to construct an 80-room hotel near the casino, with completion expected in late 2018. However, at the time of publication, construction had been slow to develop and the hotel had not been completed.

In spite of the economic boon created by the gaming business, tribes have other issues to consider in the area of gaming, as evidenced by the Abramoff Scandal.

THE ABRAMOFF SCANDAL

The Mississippi Band of Choctaw Indians, in their attempts to open their casino, got involved in a situation that led to changes in legislation regarding congressional lobbying. In 1994, the Mississippi Band of Choctaw Indians hired Jack Abramoff as a lobbyist to interact with congressional members. The Choctaw originally had lobbied the federal government directly, but after the 1994 elections, were unable to work as easily with newly elected officials. The tribe contacted Preston Gates and soon after hired the firm and Abramoff. From 1994 through 1999, the tribe paid more than $1.3 million to Abramoff and his associates.

But it wasn't just the Mississippi Band of Choctaw Indians that Abramoff was working with in relation to tribal gaming. In 2001, the Coushatta Tribe of Louisiana was interested in negotiating a 25-year compact with the state of Louisiana, and hired Abramoff as their lobbyist." The tribe agreed on March 20, 2001, to hire Abramoff at a relatively high retainer of $125,000 a month, plus expenses. In July 2001, Louisiana Governor Mike Foster approved the new gambling compact.

In October 2001, Abramoff suggested to the Louisiana Coushatta that the Texas legislature was close to legalizing certain forms of gambling in Texas. The Alabama Coushatta, a related but competing tribe, was also seeking to open a casino in eastern Texas in 2001. Because the Louisiana Coushatta attracted many customers from eastern Texas to their casino, a Texas-based Indian casino could threaten their livelihood. The opposition efforts succeeded, and Texas did not pass a bill to allow gaming.

Throughout the period, Abramoff and his associates did little more than take money from tribes to give to senior Republican politicians by creating false threats to their Indian clients (Riley, 2014/2015). Abramoff and his associates were found guilty of "fraud, tax evasion, and corrupting public officials" (Jerke, 2010, note 27). On January 3, 2006, Abramoff pleaded guilty to three felony counts—conspiracy, fraud, and tax evasion—involving charges stemming primarily from his lobbying activities in Washington on behalf of Native American tribes. According to a *Washington Post* article, Abramoff and his associates "defrauded five Native American tribes of more than $20 million" (Becker, 2011).

But it wasn't just money that the tribe lost. The Mississippi Band received a great deal of "damaging media attention" (Jones, 2008/2009) because of their association with the Abramoff scandal. After accusations surfaced of spending large sums of money lobbying Congress for the Katrina cleanup and other projects, the Choctaws looked far less appealing as a future business partner, despite the tribe's positive impact on rural Mississippi and the fact that the tribe itself was the victim of the lobbying scandal.

Thus, the Oklahoma Choctaw moved from the edge of Termination back into the status of a fully functioning tribal government. In Mississippi, the Mississippi Band of Choctaw Indians moved forward through the Bureau of Indian Affairs processes to reestablish a governing structure that had been lost more than 100 years earlier. Both governments struggled to create an economic base with which to develop their programs, but through ingenuity and perseverance, they succeeded in creating regionally strong and influential governments. In Louisiana, the Jena Band of Choctaw Indians moved toward formation of a tribal structure with the organizational structure of 1974 and its ultimate recognition as an Indian tribe in 1995.

NOTABLE FIGURES

Joseph Oklahombi

Joseph Oklahombi (Choctaw for "people killer"), a full-blood Choctaw from Bismark (present-day Wright City), Choctaw Nation, Indian Territory, was born May 1, 1895, in the Kiamichi Mountains of McCurtain County, Oklahoma. He served in the 36th Infantry Division's Company D, First Battalion, 141st Regiment, 71st Brigade during World War I.

During the October 1918 Meuse-Argonne Offensive, the U.S. Army used Choctaw soldiers of the 141st, 142nd, and 143rd Infantry Regiments, including Oklahombi, as translators in their native tongue. At headquarters they "decoded" Choctaw into English; those messages were communicated to those in the field. These Choctaw were the original "code talkers."

On October 8, 1918, at St. Etienne, France, Oklahombi played another role. He and 23 fellow soldiers attacked an enemy position and captured 171 prisoners. They seized the artillery at the site, killed 79 German soldiers, assisted the wounded in "No Man's Land," and, while under attack, held their position for four days.

It is still uncertain whether he acted alone or in partnership with his comrades, but Oklahombi was identified as "Oklahoma's Greatest Hero." He was awarded the Silver Star with the Victory Ribbon from the United States. He also received the Croix de Guerre, one of France's highest honors for gallantry, from Marshal Henri-Philippe Pétain. Despite the heroism of Oklahombi and his regimental mates, none were awarded the Medal of Honor for their valor.

After the war, Oklahombi returned to Wright City to be reunited with his wife and son. He was struck and killed by a truck as he walked along a road on April 13, 1960, and was buried with military honors in the Yashau Cemetery northwest of Broken Bow.

Muriel H. Wright

Muriel Hazel Wright (March 31, 1889—February 27, 1975) was an American teacher, historian and writer on the Choctaw Nation. Wright was born in Lehigh, Choctaw Nation, Indian Territory (now known as Lehigh, Oklahoma) in 1889. Her father was Eliphalet Wright, a Choctaw who had graduated from Union College and Albany Medical College; her grandfather was Allen Wright, who was principal chief of the Choctaw Nation from 1866 to 1870. Muriel's paternal grandmother was Harriet Newell Mitchell, a native of Dayton, Ohio, who came to Indian Territory as a Presbyterian missionary teacher and married Allen Wright in 1857. Muriel's mother was Ida Belle Richards, who was also a missionary.

Wright attended Wheaton Seminary in Norton, Massachusetts, and then completed a teacher's education course at East Central Normal School in Ada, Oklahoma, in 1912. She worked from 1912 until the mid-1920s as a teacher and as a principal in various schools in southeastern Oklahoma, taking time from 1916 to 1917 to attend Barnard College at Columbia University, where she studied English and history.

After 1924, Wright focused on research and writing. In addition to Oklahoma history textbooks *The Story of Oklahoma* (1923), *The Oklahoma History* (1929), and *Our Oklahoma* (1939), she wrote *A Guide to the Indian Tribes of Oklahoma* (1951). She co-authored, with Joseph Thoburn, a four-volume set *Oklahoma: A History of the State and its People* (1929) and with George H. Shirk and Kenny A. Franks *Mark of Heritage: Oklahoma Historical Markers* (1976).

She was very active in the Oklahoma Historical Society and served as editor of the Chronicles of Oklahoma from 1955 to 1971. In 1971, Wright was named the outstanding Indian woman of the 20th century by the North American Indian Women's Association, one among many honors she received for her accomplishments, including being named to the Oklahoma Hall of Fame in 1940 and receiving the University of Oklahoma's Distinguished Service Award in 1948; the Oklahoma City Business and Professional Woman of the Year in 1950; and an Honorary Doctor of Humane Letters from the University of Oklahoma in 1964. In 1993, she was inducted into the Oklahoma Historians Hall of Fame.

Wright was active on behalf of the Choctaw tribe, serving as a representative on its councils and working on the various economic matters involved in the transfer of tribal properties to private hands in the years following Oklahoma's statehood in 1907. In addition, she fought for just recompense for the widespread plunder of Indian Territory. Wright continued to write and plan projects until her death from a stroke in 1975 in her 86th year.

PREVIOUS CHOCTAW CHIEFS

Phillip Martin

Phillip Martin (March 13, 1926–February 4, 2010) was a former chief of the Mississippi Band of Choctaw who helped establish MBCI as the economic and political giant it is today. Martin was born in Philadelphia, Mississippi, to Willie and Mary Martin. After his father was killed by a hit-and-run driver, Phillip's mother sent Phillip to a Cherokee boarding school in North Carolina when he was 13. He enlisted in the Army at age 19, joined the Air Force after the war, and was a staff sergeant and a radar technician when discharged in 1955. He returned to the Choctaw reservation and married Bonnie Bell.

Chief Martin was first elected chief in 1979, a position he held until 2007. In the 1970s, the Choctaws in Mississippi faced an unemployment rate of nearly 75 percent, and many who had job skills had to move away from the area to pursue employment. Over the decades, those Choctaws who remained in Mississippi eked out livings through sharecropping and unskilled labor. Chief Martin changed all that with a focused program of tribal self-sufficiency and economic development.

The MBCI focused on developing its own economic programs, using a planning grant to establish a Community Action Agency; within 20 years it was administering over $10 million in grants and contracts to develop an 80-acre industrial park on the reservation. In 1981, he persuaded officials in Philadelphia, Mississippi, to issue bonds to attract the American

Greetings Card company to the industrial park. Under his leadership, the tribe started Chahta Enterprise, a multifaceted company. Through it, the tribe became an economic force in central Mississippi. It was, however, mostly through the development of the tribal gaming enterprises—the Silver Star Hotel and Casino in 1994 and a second casino, the Golden Moon, in 2002. Today they form the largest and most profitable Choctaw enterprise. According to the Harvard Project on American Indian Economic Development, the businesses have been generating about $180 million a year in wages alone. More than 7,000 people are employed, and the unemployment rate on the reservation was about 4 percent at the time of Martin's death in 2010.

Chief Martin's vision and drive changed the MBCI from a struggling cultural group with a dim economic future to the thriving social and economic force it is today.

Gregory Pyle

Gregory Pyle (born April 25, 1949) was a long-term political leader of the Choctaw Nation of Oklahoma. He was elected as principal chief in 1997 and re-elected since by wide margins. He resigned effective April 28, 2014. Prior to serving as principal chief, he had served as assistant chief to Hollis Roberts for 13 years. He began to work for the Choctaw Nation in 1975 as personnel officer. In 1983, he became a tribal program monitor to oversee the tribe's contract compliance and to ensure that all federally funded projects run by the Tribe met federal rules. In 1984, he was elected as the assistant chief of the Choctaw Nation and worked in that position until 1997, when he was elected as chief following the conviction of then-chief Hollis Roberts. He announced his resignation on his 65th birthday. Under Chief Pyle, the Choctaw Nation of Oklahoma made huge inroads into economic development, especially in the area of gaming and federal contracts.

6

❖

Choctaw in the
Contemporary World

THE CONTEMPORARY CHOCTAW
NATION OF OKLAHOMA

The tribal offices of the Choctaw Nation of Oklahoma are located in Durant, Oklahoma, although the Choctaw Capitol is located in Tuskahoma. Currently, members of the Choctaw Nation of Oklahoma live not only within the ten-and-a-half-county "service area" of southeastern Oklahoma (see District Map) but also in large metropolitan areas like Oklahoma City. In addition, as a result of the relocation policies of the 1950s, there are large groups of Choctaws in areas outside of Oklahoma, such as the Okla Chahta Clan of Bakersfield, California (www.oklachahta.org/).

According to a 2016 document created by the Oklahoma Department of Transportation in support of a Fast Lane highway improvement proposal, the service area covers roughly 10,600 square miles and more than 41,000 Choctaw tribal members (Oklahoma Department of Transportation [ODOT], 2016). Communities with large Choctaw populations include Antlers, Atoka, Broken Bow, Durant, Hugo, Idabel, and McAlester.

Tribal programs have been aimed at replacing county- and state-run programs for local populations. Tribal clinics and hospitals serve not only Choctaw members but also members of the general public and members of other tribes. Tribal language education is offered in the regional school system through a series of live-streamed televised classes, as well as throughout

CHOCTAW NATION OF OKLAHOMA DISTRICTS

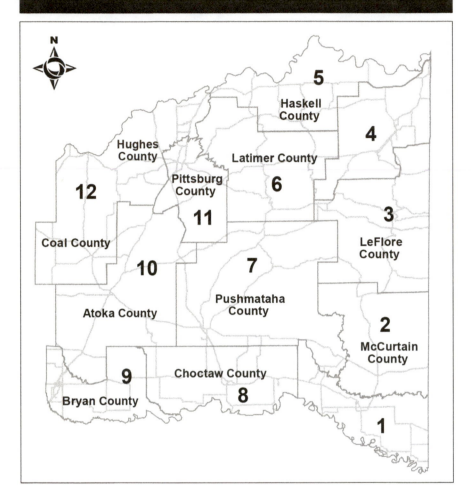

the nation on web-based learning platforms. The complexity of the tribal services is apparent through a close examination of the Choctaw Nation's website at www.choctawnation.com.

CONTEMPORARY MISSISSIPPI BAND OF CHOCTAW INDIANS

The Choctaw Indian Reservation is comprised of more than 35,000 acres in 10 different counties of Mississippi. There are currently eight communities

MISSISSIPPI CHOCTAW

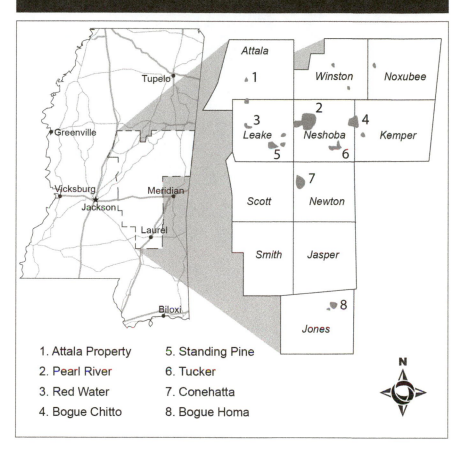

1. Attala Property
2. Pearl River
3. Red Water
4. Bogue Chitto

5. Standing Pine
6. Tucker
7. Conehatta
8. Bogue Homa

N

among the MBCI—Bogue Chitto, Bogue Homa, Conehatta, Crystal Ridge, Pearl River, Red Water, Standing Pine, and Tucker. Pearl River, in Neshoba County, is the largest community and the seat of the tribal headquarters. The 2010 federal census listed 7,471 individuals who identified as a single tribal unit, and a total of 8,979 who identified as having some combination of Mississippi Band of Choctaw Indian identification. The 2012 Tribal Profile (MBCI, 2012) indicated an enrolled tribal membership as "over 10,000, all of whom have at least a 50% blood quantum."

The tribal government continues to operate under a constitution, ratified in 1945, revised in 1975, and amended in 2006. Each of the eight tribal communities is represented in the 17-member Tribal Council—three from Conehatta, three from Bogue Chitto, and three from Pearl River, two from

Choctaw dancers in traditional clothing at the Choctaw Indian Fair, Neshoba County, Mississippi. The Choctaw Indian Fair, established in 1949, offers opportunities for visitors to learn about Choctaw culture through historical and cultural displays, social dancing, tribal arts and crafts, Choctaw stickball, and traditional Choctaw food. (Natalie Maynor)

Red Water, two from Tucker, and two from Red Water; and one each from the Bogue Homa and Crystal Ridge communities. The Tribal Council has the legislative and policy-making authority, and its members are elected on staggered four-year terms. The tribal chief is the tribe's principal executive officer, and is elected to a four-year term with no term limits. In July 2011, Phyliss J. Anderson was recognized as the MBCI fourth chief and first female MBCI tribal chief.

One thing of lasting importance to the MBCI is the Choctaw Indian Fair. Begun in 1949, the Fair highlighted Mississippi Choctaw arts and crafts, culture, and history, and gave people the opportunity to renew acquaintances, make new ones, and highlight tribal accomplishments.

The Tribal website, www.choctaw.org, offers a broad range of information on contemporary tribal issues, programs, and other information, and should be checked on a regular basis. It has not been updated recently, however, and information might be lacking. For example, the most recent press release was dated April 10, 2017.

Peterson (1992) summarizes the MBCI development from the 1960s and 1970s: "Not until 1979 did economic development become the top priority of the Choctaw tribal government . . . Initially, from 1964 to 1971, a major

---

CHOCTAW FESTIVALS

The Mississippi Band of Choctaw Indians started the Choctaw Indian Fair in 1949 as an opportunity for people to renew acquaintances, celebrate Choctaw culture, and reconnect with family. As noted in the tribal website (www.choc tawindianfair.com/index.html), the fair takes place every July in Choctaw, Mississippi. The year 2018 marks the 69th annual Choctaw Indian Fair. Fairgoers experience historical and cultural displays, social dancing, tribal arts and crafts, Choctaw stickball, the Choctaw Indian Princess Pageant, and traditional Choctaw food. The fair also offers carnival rides and games, and performances each night.

In 2018, the Choctaw Nation of Oklahoma will hold its 68th annual Labor Day Festival on the Capital grounds in Tuskahoma, Oklahoma. The Choctaw Labor Day Festival, begun in 1950, offers attendees arts, entertainment, sports (softball, basketball, and stickball), cultural activities (such as Choctaw dances, the Little Miss, Junior Miss, and Miss Choctaw Nation of Oklahoma pageants), Choctaw food, an intertribal powwow, and other family fun. Held in the final month of summer, for the southeast quarter of the state, it is one of the most anticipated events of the year, drawing an estimated crowd of nearly 100,000 people.

In October 2018, the Jena Band of Choctaw Indians hosted its 10th Annual Jena Choctaw Pow Wow in the Pines at the Jena Band of Choctaw Pow Wow Grounds next to the tribal office in Trout, Louisiana. The Jena Choctaw Pow Wow in the Pines is an annual celebration of the federal recognition of the Jena Band of Choctaw Indians, typically held the second full weekend (Friday and Saturday) of October.

---

effort had been made to address social issues and needs. From 1972 to 1979 a major effort had been to strengthen tribal government" (p. 154).

CONTEMPORARY JENA BAND OF CHOCTAW INDIANS

The contemporary Jena Band of Indians still occupies the general area of Louisiana that they have lived in since the 1880s. According to the Jena tribal website, there were 327 tribal members (Jena Band, 2015).

As noted in chapter 5, tribal economic development centers primarily on the Choctaw Pines Casino, although the tribes does operate a retail wine, beer, and spirits store known as Twisted Feather, and a day care/child care center known as Baby Feathers.

The tribal website at www.jenachoctaw.org offers glimpses into the programs offered by the tribe for the benefit of its members, including

JENA BAND OF CHOCTAW INDIANS

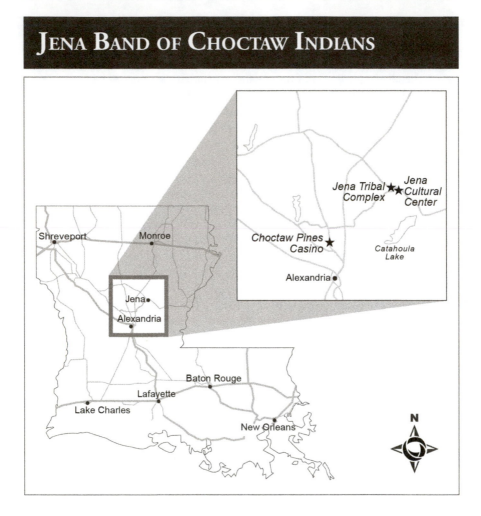

education, health, social services, housing, and transportation programs. The Tribe established its Environmental Department (funded by a U.S. Environmental Protection Agency General Assistance Program grant) in November 2000 to develop environmental programs that protect human health and natural resources for the Jena Band of Choctaw Indians. Additionally, the tribe has been formally recognized by the National Park Service as eligible to take over some of the responsibilities of the State of Louisiana's Historic Preservation Office under the National Historic Preservation Act. Their Tribal Historic Preservation Office was established in 2010.

The three federally recognized tribes of Choctaws are moving forward based on a shared history. However, there are other groups of people who have a similar shared history and yet are not recognized by the federal government as a formal American Indian tribe with a government-to-government relationship with the federal government.

FEDERALLY RECOGNIZED VERSUS NONFEDERALLY RECOGNIZED TRIBES

Indian tribe is defined as "an Indian tribe, band, nation, or other organized group or community, including a Native village, Regional Corporation or Village Corporation (as those terms are defined in section 3 of the Alaska Native Claims Settlement Act [43 USC 1602]) that is recognized as eligible for the special programs and services provided by the United States to Indians because of their status as Indians." Therefore, the term *Indian tribe* refers to federally recognized Indian tribes. The federal government has a unique political and legal relationship with Indian tribes—a trust responsibility—not shared by nonfederally recognized tribes. The federal government works with Indian tribes on a nation-to-nation basis.

The term *nonfederally recognized tribe* is not defined on a national level and can include state-recognized tribes and tribal entities without state or federal recognition. Often, tribal entities without state recognition are still recognized by national Indian organizations and intertribal coalitions. For example, National Congress of American Indians (NCAI) membership includes federally recognized and nonfederally recognized tribes. Additionally, many federally recognized tribes have strong and long-standing relationships and kinship ties with nonfederally recognized tribes and recognize them as tribes.

Federally recognized tribes are recognized as possessing certain inherent rights of self-government (i.e., tribal sovereignty) and are entitled to receive certain federal benefits, services, and protections because of their special relationship with the United States. As of May 1, 2018, there were 573 federally recognized American Indian and Alaska Native tribes and villages.

CLIFTON-CHOCTAW

Klopotek describes the chance meeting of two Choctaw speakers in a hospital room in Alexandria, Louisiana, in 1976, as the impetus for the organization of a community of Choctaw in Clifton, Rapides Parish, Louisiana (2011). Following the 1977 incorporation of the Clifton-Choctaw tribal council as a nonprofit entity—the Clifton-Choctaw Reservation, Inc.—the quest for tribal recognition began. As a group associated strongly with the timber industry, once the logging trucks were gone, unemployment and poverty crept in (Klopotek, 2011).

The groups submitted a letter of intent to petition the Bureau of Indian Affairs for federal recognition in March of 1978, and in April of the same year, received recognition from the Louisiana legislature as a state-recognized tribe. However, legal concerns by the state's attorney general, William J. Guste Jr. led the Senate to change the bill to concede that the state acknowledged only "the presence of a self-proclaimed Indian community" and nullified language from the bill urging federal recognition (Klopotek, 2011, p. 202).

According to Klopotek, the Clifton-Choctaw and other Choctaw communities that were trying to follow the federal-recognition maze at the time (including the Choctaw-Apaches) were seen by some people as "'really' white, Latino, or black" trying to "pass" as Indian either to cash in on the casino boom or to improve their racial status. Others saw them as "Indian," but perhaps with such mixed ancestry to make determination of them as a "tribe" difficult (Klopotek, 2011, p. 203).

Genealogical issues with some of the Clifton-Choctaw families created problems for the Office of Federal Acknowledgment (OFA) in its recognition process. Klopotek (2011) discusses the issues associated with African heritage issues in Louisiana (and the southern United States in general), working from those issues to offer justifications for exclusion and/or inclusion, noting, "it is far easier for a black Indian enrolled in a federally recognized tribe to be accepted as a Indian than it is for a black Indian from a nonfederal tribe" (p. 215). To others, *not* standing up as "Indian" was similarly unacceptable.

Klopotek documents the Clifton-Choctaw choices to attend "white" schools (thereby tacitly identifying themselves politically as "white") rather than attend "colored" schools during the days of the deeply segregated South. He further notes that, in Louisiana, Indians could be considered white for many purposes, and that a person classified as white could have some Indian ancestry and still be considered white, whereas a person with known African ancestry would not typically be considered so.

The tribal center constructed with federal funds offers a location where the Clifton-Choctaw participate in community events that tie them together. Whether or not federal recognition occurs in the near future, the processes undertaken to meet recognition requirements have created cohesion in the members of the community. The groups have used grants to improve housing, educational support, and cultural programs. Federal recognition would bring more opportunities, but the Clifton-Choctaw are not waiting until it does (or doesn't) happen to move forward.

THE FEDERAL RECOGNITION PROCESS

In order to achieve status as a federally recognized tribe, a petitioner has to provide documentation to the OFA that the group meets *all* seven of the following criteria spelled out in 25 CFR, Part 83:

1. The petitioner has been identified as an American Indian entity on a substantially continuous basis since 1900;

2. The petitioner comprises a distinct community and demonstrates that it existed as a community from 1900 until the present;

3. The petitioner has maintained political influence or authority over its members as an autonomous entity from 1900 until the present;

4. The petitioner must provide a copy of the entity's present governing document, including its membership criteria; or in the absence of a governing document, a written statement describing in full its membership criteria and current governing procedures;

5. The petitioner's membership consists of individuals who descend from a historical Indian tribe (or from historical Indian tribes that combined and functioned as a single autonomous political entity);

6. The petitioner's membership is composed principally of persons who are not members of any federally recognized Indian tribe; and

7. Neither the petitioner nor its members are the subject of congressional legislation that has expressly terminated or forbidden the Federal relationship. (OFA, 1997)

Failure to meet the requirements in any one of these criteria forces the assistant secretary of Indian Affairs to deny recognition to the petitioner.

Petitioners begin the process by sending a letter of intent to the assistant secretary of Indian Affairs signed by their leaders. Following this, the OFA provides a packet of information that includes the seven criteria as well as suggestions concerning the process for putting their petition packet together. The tribe then gathers and submits the information for review by anthropologists, historians, and other staff in order to evaluate the petitioner's claim.

The BIA's Branch of Acknowledgment and Research reviews the documentation and decides whether the tribe is ready to proceed. If deemed unready by the BAR, tribes have an unlimited amount of time to assemble additional documentation. If deemed ready, the tribe's petition moves into "active consideration."

Following official consideration, the tribe receives an initial conclusion, called a "proposed finding." The development of this proposed finding step can take up to a year. Once the proposed finding is received, the tribe and the public have the opportunity to respond to the initial finding during a commentary period.

During this time, the BIA researchers prepare a recommendation, taking into account the petitioners' response to the finding, as well as public comments. That recommendation takes into consideration the material provided by the tribal petitioner, as well as comments made by outside "interested parties." The interested parties many include members of the general public, local governmental entities, or other tribal groups.

Finally, the assistant secretary will determine whether to accept the petition. Tribes who don't like the outcome can appeal their case through the Interior Board of Indian Appeals or sue in federal court.

If the petitioner decides not to pursue the decision through appeal of through federal court, one other mechanism whereby groups can get federal recognition is through a legislative process. In January 2018, six Virginia state-recognized tribes obtained recognition through the Thomasina E. Jordan Indian Tribes of Virginia Federal Recognition Act of 2017, signed into law on January 29, 2018.

THE MOWA

The term MOWA is an acronym developed out of the geographic areas where this group lives—Montgomery and Washington counties—in south Alabama. According to Jacqueline Matte (2006), the MOWA Choctaws are descendants of Native Americans who occupied this territory prior to European discovery. They are situated in an area straddling the county line between south Washington County and north Mobile County in a community wedged between the small southwest Alabama towns of Citronelle, Mount Vernon, and McIntosh. Matte describes them as descendants of Choctaw Indians who fought on the side of the Creeks in the Creek War of 1813–1814, as well as those who remained in the area after most members of their nation traveled west during the Indian removal of the 1830s.

According to Matte (2006), the Choctaw groups from which the MOWA claim descent have been documented in the Mobile area since after the Creek War, becoming, in Matte's words, "fugitives in their own lands when the Treaty of Dancing Rabbit Creek took away their lands and turned them into squatters" (p. 178). After the Civil War, when many of the Choctaw men had been enlisted into the Confederate Army as scouts, the community lived in relative isolation for the surrounding population.

As was mentioned in relation to the Clifton-Choctaw, anyone not listed as "white" chose to sink into the background rather than be counted as "black." Still, the group persisted and, in 1979, was recognized by the state of Alabama. It opened its first tribal office in 1980 and undertook the work of seeking federal recognition through the Bureau of Indian Affairs' (BIA) Bureau of Acknowledgment and Research (BAR).

The MOWA did not receive acknowledgment. According to the BIA's letter of denial (OFA, 1997), "no evidence was found to demonstrate that the ancestors of the petitioner were descended from a single historic tribe or tribes which combined and functioned as an autonomous entity" (p. 5). According to the denial document, the MOWA Band's petition failed to meet acknowledgment requirements because:

(1) The petitioner's core ancestral families did not document American Indian ancestry;

(2) The families which are the actual MOWA progenitors from 1880 have not been documented as descendants of the known removal-era, antebellum American Indians claimed as ancestors by the petitioner;

(3) Many of the early nineteenth century persons claimed as members of their "founding Indian community" by the petitioner cannot be demonstrated to be Choctaw, or even American Indian; and

(4) Only one percent of the petitioner's membership can document American Indian ancestry. This ancestry comes through other ancestral lines than those going to the two core families (OFA, 1997).

According to the BIA, the only *documented* ancestry entered into the group in the 1880s and early 1900s through marriage, and only 1 percent of the MOWA trace ancestry to these lines. The BIA Denial packet also contains other material rebutting that submitted by the MOWA.

Matte argues that nonrecognition hinges on the isolation of the group, the opposition of recognition by the leaders of the Poarch Band Creeks and the Mississippi Choctaw based on their fear that the MOWA might initiate gaming. Matte offers other arguments as well, especially that "the MOWA ancestors who lived as a separate community in the mid- to late nineteenth century cannot be documented according to BAR guidelines through records produced by the non-Indian people who persecuted them" (p. 198).

As of this writing, the MOWA are still not federally recognized. Congressman Jo Bonner, of the Alabama first district, has offered congressional resolutions to extend recognition to the MOWA, more recently in the *Mowa Band of Choctaw Indians Recognition Act* (H.R. 766) in the 112th Congress on February 17, 2011.

ISLE DE JEAN CHARLES BAND

Another group of people has been billed as the "First American 'Climate Refugees.'" The Isle de Jean Charles Band of the Biloxi-Chitimacha-Choctaw Confederated of Muskogees (BCCM) is part of an alliance of three ancestrally related state-recognized groups located in Terrebonne and Lafourch parishes. Members of the Isle de Jean Charles Band, more specifically, are located on the margins of Bayou St. Jean Charles in an area now experiencing rapid sea-level rise as a result of global climate change. The *New York Times* (Davenport & Robertson, 2016) reported on the situation as "a lost cause." On December 17, 2017, Tristan Baurick of the *New Orleans Times-Picayune* reported that the Isle de Jean Charles residents who choose to relocate will be settled on a sugar farm outside of Houma, Louisiana.

CONCLUSION

It's difficult to write a "concluding" chapter on the Choctaw. These are communities of people who spoke a shared language and have a fractionated and shared history. They have continued to exist—whether within the public (and governmental) eye or "hiding in plain sight"—until leaders recognize the need to move into more formal relations with the federal government. Some are actively pursuing the social, political, and economic benefits that might come with federal recognition, while others continue to wait. One thing these groups have in common is the belief that no one can tell an individual whether he or she is Indian or not. Federal recognition is a tool that allows tribal governance more opportunities for development—it is not a panacea that cures societal ills.

The Trail(s) of Tears that the ancestors of the Choctaw Nation of Oklahoma took created a shared experience that galvanized Choctaw individuals into a nation forged by adversity, yet willing to move strongly forward. In spite of the federal government's attempts to "terminate" its relationship with the Nation, reestablishment of Choctaw governance in the 1970s created a strong force in southeastern Oklahoma. Today, the Choctaw Nation of Oklahoma celebrates its history through strong cultural connections.

The Choctaw who chose not to remove to Oklahoma, but to stay in Mississippi, underwent another history, one that required them to give up their broad tribal governance. Until such time as it was possible and feasible to reemerge as the Mississippi Band of Choctaw Indians, the group never gave up its Indian identity. It reorganized in order to recreate a governance structure, and developed programs that increased social, financial, and service-oriented opportunities for the Band. Today, the Mississippi Band of Choctaw Indians is one of the strongest economic forces in Mississippi.

The Jena Band, as the smallest of the federally recognized groups, is also the "newest" in terms of political age. The Jena, by surviving the federal acknowledgment process, have truly just begun to flex their economic and political muscle. It remains to be seen how the group will prosper and the ways that its members will benefit from its opportunities.

At this point in time, the nonrecognized groups still operate within an uncertain status. They have a shared history, shared relatives and ancestors, and they are "Indian." Yet, they can't seem to prove to the federal government that they are historically "Indian enough" to regain the special relationship between the federal government and themselves. In this regard, truly, only time will tell.

NOTABLE FIGURES

Clara Sue Kidwell

Clara Sue Kidwell (born July 8, 1941) is an academic scholar, historian, feminist, and Native American author of White Earth Chippewa and Choctaw descent, and is considered to be a major figure in the development of American Indian studies programs.

Kidwell was born in Tahlequah, Oklahoma, in 1941, and grew up in Muskogee, Oklahoma. In 1959, Kidwell graduated from Central High School and went on to attend the University of Oklahoma, where she earned her bachelor's degree in 1963. She was a member of the University's College Bowl Team, which led to her receiving a fellowship in the history of science after she graduated with her bachelor's degree. She earned her master's in 1966 and her PhD in 1970, both also from the University of Oklahoma.

In 1970, Kidwell taught at Haskell Indian Junior College (now Haskell Indian Nations University), where she worked for two years. She left to be an associate professor at the University of California at Berkeley, where she worked until 1993, with a stint as a visiting scholar and associate professor at Dartmouth College in 1980. After Berkeley, she took her career in a new direction as the assistant director for cultural resources at the National Museum of the American Indian, where she helped move 1 million different pieces from the George Gustav Heye's Museum of the American Indian from New York to Washington, DC.

In 1995, she chose to return to the University of Oklahoma and accepted a tenured position as the founding director of the Native American studies program, which she crafted into a leading program in the field of Native American studies.

In 2007, Kidwell left the University of Oklahoma to start the American Indian Center (AIC) at the University of North Carolina (UNC). Under Kidwell's leadership, AIC has had success in North Carolina, increasing programs that address education, health, and child welfare for federally unrecognized tribes. Kidwell retired from her position as director of AIC in June 2011.

Kidwell has authored numerous articles, but also the following books: *The Choctaws in Oklahoma: From Tribe to Nation, 1855–1970* (2008); *Native American Studies* (with Alan Velie in 2005); with Homer Noley and George Tinker (2001) *A Native American Theology*; *Choctaws and Missionaries in Mississippi, 1818–1918* in 1997; and with Charles Roberts (in 1980) *The Choctaws: A Critical Bibliography*.

CURRENT CHOCTAW CHIEFS

Gary Batton

Gary Batton, chief of the Choctaw Nation of Oklahoma (2014–). The Choctaw Nation of Oklahoma has elected its own chief only since 1971. Prior to 1971, chiefs were appointed by the president of the United States. As with previously elected chiefs, Batton seeks to increase the Choctaw Nation's economic self-sufficiency and improve member benefits. (U.S. Department of Agriculture)

Gary Dale Batton (born December 15, 1966) is the current and 47th chief of the Choctaw Nation of Oklahoma. Batton began working for the Choctaw Nation in 1987 in the Purchasing Department as a clerk. He became deputy director of the Choctaw Nation Housing Authority in 1989 after he received his bachelor's degree in business management from Southeastern Oklahoma State University in Durant, Oklahoma; executive director of the Choctaw Nation Health Services Authority in 1997; and on the resignation of Assistant Chief Mike Bailey in May 2007, he was selected and served as assistant chief. He served in that position until the retirement of Chief Gregory E. Pyle in April 2014, after which Batton was appointed chief. He was elected chief in the general election on July 11, 2015, for a four-year term ending on September 2, 2019.

Phyliss J. Anderson

Phyliss Anderson (born January 1, 1961) was elected in 2011 as the current chief of the Mississippi Band of Choctaw Indians. She was raised in the Red Water community of Leake County, Mississippi, with six sisters. She started working for the MBCI as a receptionist and payroll clerk at Choctaw Development Enterprise until recruited by the late Chief Phillip Martin as an executive assistant. She worked her way through the tribal government programs and eventually landed a position as the director of Natural Resources.

In 2003, she ran for elected office as a council representative from her community of Red Water. She was elected and served eight years on the tribal council, including four years as secretary-treasurer. She was elected as the first female chief of the MBCI in 2011, and reelected to a second term in 2015.

B. Cheryl Smith

B. Cheryl Smith (born 1954) began working for the tribe just after graduating from Jena High School in 1972. She was very instrumental during the tribe's federal recognition process, serving as tribal secretary, collecting information and history for the submission process. She was elected and served as council under Chief Jerry Jackson, and was elected as the first woman chief of the Jena Band in 1998 for a four-year term. She was again elected in 2010 and is now serving her third term as tribal chief. In 2011, the tribe opened its first enterprise, Twisted Feathers, followed by Baby Feathers Day Care and Learning Center in 2014, and finally Jena Choctaw Pines Casino.

References

Adair, James. 2013 (1775). *The History of the American Indians; Particularly Those Nations Adjoining to the Mississippi, East and West Florida, Georgia, South and North Carolina, and Virginia.* Cambridge: Cambridge University Press.

Albright, Caroline H. 1983. "The Summerville IV Community." In *Excavations in the Lubbub Creek Archaeological Locality: Prehistoric Agricultural Communities in West Central Alabama,* vol. 1, edited by Christopher Peebles (pp. 309–390). Unpublished report submitted to the U.S. Army Corps of Engineers, Mobile, AL. Manuscript on file with the Office of Archaeological Research, Moundville, AL.

Amick, Daniel S., and Philip J. Carr. 1996. "Changing Strategies of Lithic Technological Organization." In *Archaeology of the Mid-Holocene Southeast,* edited by Kenneth E. Sassaman and David G. Anderson (pp. 41–56). Gainesville: University of Florida Press.

Anderson, David G., and Glen T. Hanson. 1988. "Early Archaic Settlement in the Southeastern United States: A Case Study from the Savannah River Basin." *American Antiquity* 53: 262–286.

Anderson, David G., and Kenneth E. Sassaman. 2004. "Early and Middle Holocene periods, 9500–3750 BC." In *Handbook of North American Indians,* vol. 14: *Southeast,* edited by Raymond D. Fogelson (pp. 77–87). Washington, DC: Smithsonian Institution.

"Barfoot, Van T." 2008. Medal of Honor Recipients; World War II. U.S. Army Center of Military History. Available at https://history.army.mil/html /moh/wwII-a-f.html#BARFOOT.

Baird, W. David. 1973. *The Choctaw People*. Phoenix, AZ: Indian Tribal Series.

Barsh, Russel Lawrence. 1991. "American Indians in the Great War." *Ethnohistory* 38, no. 3: 276–303.

Bartram, William. 1791. *Travels Through North & South Carolina, Georgia, East & West Florida, the Cherokee Country, the Extensive Territories of the Muscogulges, or Creek Confederacy, and the Country of the Chactaws; Containing An Account of the Soil and Natural Productions of Those Regions, Together with Observations on the Manners of the Indians*. Embellished with Copper-Plates. Philadelphia, PA: James & Johnson.

Baurick, Tristan. 2017. "Here's Where Residents of Sinking Isle de Jean Charles Will Relocate." *The Times-Picayune*, December 19, 2017. Available at https://www.nola.com/environment/index.ssf/2017/12/site_chosen _ for_relocating_isl.html.

Bearss, Edwin C. 1969. "Fort Smith as the Agency for the Western Choctaws." *The Arkansas Historical Quarterly* 27, no. 1: 40–58.

Beck, M. W. 1996. "On Discerning the Cause of Late Pleistocene Megafaunal Extinctions." *Paleobiology* 22: 91–103.

Becker, Amanda. 2011. "Legal briefs: Abramoff Accomplice Sentenced." *Washington Post*, February 14. Available at http://www.washingtonpost.com /wp-dyn/content/article/2011/02/11/AR2011021106027.html?noredirect=on.

Bense, Judith A. 1994. *Archaeology of the Southeastern United States*. San Diego, CA: Academic Press.

Blitz, John H. 1983. "Pre-Mississippian Communities." In *Excavations in the Lubbub Creek Archaeological Locality: Prehistoric Agricultural Communities in West Central Alabama*, vol. 1, edited by Christopher Peebles (pp. 198–253). Unpublished report submitted to the U.S. Army Corps of Engineers, Mobile, AL. Manuscript on file with the Office of Archaeological Research, Moundville, AL.

Blitz, John H. 1993. *Ancient Chiefdoms of the Tombigbee*. Tuscaloosa: University of Alabama Press.

Bossu, Jean B. 1771. *Travels through That Part of North American Formerly Called Louisiana*. Translated from the French by Johann Reinhold Forster. London: Davies.

Bounds, Thelma V. 1964. *Children of Nanih Waiya*. San Antonio, TX: Naylor.

Bowes, John P. 2014. "American Indian Removal beyond the Removal Act." *Native American and Indigenous Studies* 1, no. 1: 65–87.

Bradley, Bruce, and Dennis Stanford. 2004. "The North Atlantic Ice-Edge Corridor: a Possible Paleolithic Route to the New World." *World Archaeology* 36: 459–478.

Brain, Jeffrey P. 1985. "Introduction." *Final Report of the United States De Soto Expedition Commission.* United States De Soto Expedition Commission. Washington, DC: Smithsonian Institution.

Brain, Jeffery, and Philip Phillips. 1996. *Shell Gorgets: Styles of the Late Prehistoric and Protohistoric Southeast.* Cambridge, MA: Peabody Museum of Archaeology and Ethology, Harvard University.

Braje, Todd J., Tom D. Dillehay, Jon M. Erlandson, Scott M. Fitzpatrick, Donald K. Grayson, Vance T. Holliday, Robert L. Kelly, Richard G. Klein, David J. Meltzer, and Torben C. Rick. 2017. "Were Hominins in California ~130,000 Years Ago?" *Paleoamerica* 3, no. 3, 200–202.

Brescia, William, ed. 1982. *Tribal Government: A New Era.* Philadelphia, MS: Choctaw Heritage Press, Mississippi Band of Choctaw Indians.

Brown, Ian W. 2004. "The History of the Gulf Coastal Plain After 500 BC." In *Handbook of North American Indians,* vol. 14: *Southeast,* edited by Raymond D. Fogelson (pp. 575–585). Washington, DC: Smithsonian Institution.

Bushnell, David, Jr. 1909. "The Choctaw Indians of Bayou Lacomb, St. Tammany Parish, Louisiana." *Smithsonian Institution Bureau of American Ethnology Bulletin* 48. Washington, DC: Government Printing Office.

Byington, Cyrus. 1915. *A Dictionary of the Choctaw Language.* Washington: Bureau of American Ethnology, vol. 46.

Caddell, Gloria. 1981. "Plant Resources, Archaeological Plant Remains, and Prehistoric Plant-Use Patterns in the Central Tombigbee River Valley." In *Biocultural Studies in the Gainesville Lake Area of the Tennessee-Tombigbee Waterway,* by Gloria Caddell, Anne Woodrick, and Mary C. Hill (pp. 1–90). *Archaeological Investigations in the Gainesville Lake Area of Tennessee-Tombigbee Waterway,* vol. 4, Report of Investigations 14. Office of Archaeological Research, University of Alabama, Tuscaloosa.

Caddell, Gloria. 1983. "Floral Remains from the Lubbub Creek Archaeological Locality." In *Excavations in the Lubbub Creek Archaeological Locality: Prehistoric Agricultural Communities in West Central Alabama,* vol. 2, edited by Christopher Peebles (pp. 194–217). Report on file with Office of Archaeological Research, Moundville, AL.

Carleton, Kenneth H. 1994. "Where did the Choctaw Come From? An Examination of Pottery in Areas Adjacent to the Choctaw Homeland." In *Perspectives on the Southeast: Linguistics, Archaeology, and Ethnohistory,* edited by Patricia B. Kwachka. Southern Anthropological Society Proceedings, No. 27. Athens: University of Georgia Press.

Carleton, Kenneth H. 2002. "A Brief History of the Mississippi Band of Choctaw Indians." Mississippi Archaeological Association. Available at http://www.msarchaeology.org/maa/carleton.pdf.

Carson, James Taylor. 1997. "Native Americans, the Market Revolution, and Culture Change: The Choctaw Cattle Economy, 1690–1830." *Agricultural History* 71, no. 1: 1–18.

Catlin, George. 2001 (1844). *Letters and Notes on the Manners, Customs, and Conditions of the North American Indians: Written during Eight Years' Travel (1832–1839) amongst the Wildest Tribes of Indians in North America*, vol. 2. Scituate, MA: DSI Digital Pub Group.

Champagne, Duane. 1992. *Social Order and Political Change: Constitutional Governments Among the Cherokee, the Choctaw, the Chickasaw, and the Creek*. Stanford, CA: Stanford University Press.

Chapman, Jefferson. 1999. *Tellico Archaeology*, rev. ed. Knoxville: Tennessee Valley Authority.

Choctaw Nation. 1838. "1838 October Choctaw Nation Constitution." Available at https://www.choctawnation.com/sites/default/files/2015/09/29/1838constitution_original.pdf.

Choctaw Nation of Oklahoma. n.d. Homepage. www.choctawnation.com.

Claiborne, John. 1880. *Mississippi as a Province, Territory, and State: With Biographical Notices of Eminent Citizens*, vol. 1. Jackson, MS: Power and Barksdale.

Clark, Blue. 2009. *Indian Tribes of Oklahoma: A Guide*. Civilization of the American Indian Series, vol. 261. Norman: University of Oklahoma Press.

Clark, Donald W. 1991. "The Northern (Alaska-Yukon) Fluted Points." In *Clovis: Origins and Adaptations*, edited by Robson Bonnichsen and Karen L. Turnmire (pp. 35–49). Corvallis: Peopling of the Americas Publications, Center for the Study of the First Americans, Oregon State University.

Clayton, Lawrence A., Vernon James Knight Jr., and Edward C. Moore. 1993. *The De Soto Chronicles: The Expedition of Hernando De Soto in North America in 1539–1543*, vols. 1 & 2. Tuscaloosa: University of Alabama Press.

Cole, Gloria. 1983. "Environmental Background." In *Excavations in the Lubbub Creek Archaeological Locality: Prehistoric Agricultural Communities in West Central Alabama*, vol. 1, edited by Christopher Peebles (pp. 10–63). Report on file with the Office of Archaeological Research, Moundville, AL.

Cole, Gloria, and Caroline H. Albright. 1983. "Summerville I–II Fortifications." In *Excavations in the Lubbub Creek Archaeological Locality:*

Prehistoric Agricultural Communities in West Central Alabama, vol. 1, edited by Christopher Peebles (pp. 140–196). Report on file with the Office of Archaeological Research, Moundville, AL.

Cottrell, Steve. 1998. *Civil War in the Indian Territory*. Gretna, LA: Pelican.

Crites, Gary. 1993. "Domesticated Sunflower in Fifth Millennium B.P. Temporal Context: New Evidence from Middle Tennessee." *American Antiquity* 58: 146–148.

Cushman, Henry B. 1899. *History of the Choctaw, Chickasaw, and Natchez Indians*. New York: Russell & Russell.

Davenport, Coral, and Campbell Robertson. 2016. "Resettling the First American 'Climate Refugees.'" *The New York Times*, May 3, 2016. Available at https://www.nytimes.com/2016/05/03/us/resettling-the-first-american-climate-refugees.html.

The Dearborn Independent. 1921. "Briefly Told." November 5, 1921, p. 16.

Debo, Angie. (1934) 1961. *The Rise and Fall of the Choctaw Republic*. Civilization of the American Indian Series, vol. 6. Norman: University of Oklahoma.

Debo, Angie. (1940) 1968. *And Still the Waters Run: The Betrayal of the Five Civilized Tribes*. Princeton, NJ: Princeton University Press.

DeRosier, Arthur H. Jr. 1970. *The Removal of the Choctaw Indians*. New York: Harper and Row.

Dillehay Thomas D. 1989. *Monte Verde: A Late Pleistocene Settlement in Chile, vol. 1: The Paleo-Environment and Site Context*. Washington, DC: Smithsonian Institution Press.

Dillehay Thomas D. 1997. *Monte Verde: A Late Pleistocene Settlement in Chile, vol. 2: The Archaeological Context*. Washington, DC: Smithsonian Institution Press.

Dillehay, Tom D., Carlos Ocampo, José Saavedra, Andre Oliveira Sawakuchi, Rodrigo M. Vega, Mario Pino, Michael B. Collins, et al. 2015. "New Archaeological Evidence for an Early Human Presence at Monte Verde, Chile." PLoS One, November 18. Available at https://doi.org/10.1371/journal.pone.0141923.

Dixon, James E. 1999. *Bones, Boats, and Bison: Archaeology and the First Colonization of Western North America*. Albuquerque: University of New Mexico Press.

Doran, Glen. 1992. "Problems and Potential of Wet Sites in North America: The Example of Windover." In *The Wetland Revolution in Prehistory*, edited by Bryony Coles (pp. 125–134). Proceedings of a conference held by the Prehistory Society and WARP at the University of Exeter, April 1991.

Doran, Michael F. 1975. "Population Statistics of the Nineteenth Century Indian Territory." *Chronicles of Oklahoma* 53: 492–515.

Du Pratz, Antoine Simon Le Page. (1758) 2005. *History of Louisiana: Or of the Western Parts of Virginia and Carolina* . . . Farmington Hills, MI: Thomson Gale.

Dupumeux. 1751. "Letter to Beauchamp, June 18, 1751." In Rowland, Dunbar and Albert G. Sanders, *Mississippi Provincial Archives: French Dominion* 5: 89–90.

Elvas, a Gentleman from (1557) 1993. True Relation of the Hardships Suffered by Governor Hernando De Soto and Certain Portuguese Gentlemen During the Discovery of the Province of Florida. [1557]. Transl. by James Alexander Robinson. In *The De Soto Chronicles: The Expedition of Hernando De Soto to North America in 1539–1543*, vol. 1, edited by Lawrence Clayton, Vernon James Knight Jr., and Edward C. Moore (pp. 19–220). Tuscaloosa: University of Alabama Press.

Ensor, H. Blaine. 1980. An Evaluation of the Synthesis of Changing Lithic Technologies in the Central Tombigbee Valley. *Southeastern Archaeological Conference Bulletin* 22: 83–90.

Ensor, H. Blaine. 1981. Gainesville Lake Area Lithics: Chronology, Technology and Use. In *Archaeological Investigations of the Gainesville Lake Area of the Tennessee-Tombigbee Waterway*, vol. 3, University of Alabama Office of Archaeological Research.

Erlandson, Jon M. 2001. The Archaeology of Aquatic Adaptations: Paradigms for a New Millennium. *Journal of Archaeological Research* 9: 287–350.

Fagan, Brian M. 2000. *Ancient North America: The Archaeology of a Continent*. London: Thames & Hudson.

Faiman-Silva, Sandra. 1997. *Choctaws at the Crossroads: The Political Economy of Class and Culture in the Oklahoma Timber Region*. Lincoln: University of Nebraska Press.

Fiedel, Stuart. 2000. "The Peopling of the New World: Present Evidence, New Theories, and Future Directions." *Journal of Archaeological Research* 8: 39–103.

Foreman, Carolyn Thomas. 1943. *Indians Abroad, 1493–1938*. Civilization of the American Indian Series, vol. 24. Norman: University of Oklahoma.

Foreman, Grant. 1976. *Indian Removal: The Emigration of the Five Civilized Tribes of Indians*. Civilization of the American Indian Series, vol. 2. Norman: University of Oklahoma Press.

Galloway, Patricia K. 1995. *Choctaw Genesis 1500–1700*. Indians of the Southeast Series. Lincoln: University of Nebraska Press.

Galloway, Patricia, and Clara Sue Kidwell. 2004. "Choctaw in the East." In *Handbook of North American Indians*, vol. 14: *Southeast*, edited by Raymond Fogelson (pp. 499–519). Washington, DC: Smithsonian Institution.

Gantt, Sean E. 2013. *Nanta Hosh Chahta Immi?* (What Are Choctaw Lifeways?): Cultural Preservation in the Casino Era. Unpublished dissertation. http://digitalrepository.unm.edu/anth_etds/25.

Garcilaso de la Vega. [1596] 1993. "La Florida." Transl. by Charmion Shelby. In *The De Soto Chronicles: The Expedition of Hernando De Soto to North America in 1539–1543*, edited by Lawrence A. Clayton, Vernon James Knight Jr., and Edward C. Moore (pp. 25–560). Tuscaloosa: University of Alabama Press.

Gibson, Arrell M. 1965. *Oklahoma: A History of Five Centuries*. Oklahoma City, OK: Harlow.

Gibson, Jon L., and J. Richard Shenkel. 1989. "Louisiana Earthworks: Middle Woodland and Predecessors." In *Middle Woodland Settlement and Ceremonialism in the Midsouth and Lower Mississippi Valley*, edited by R. C. Mainfort Jr. (pp. 7–18). Jackson: Mississippi Department of Archives and History.

Goebel, Ted, Roger Powers, and Nancy Bilge. 1991. "The Nennana Complex of Alaska and Clovis Origins." In *Clovis: Origins and Adaptations*, edited by Robson Bonnichsen and Karen L. Turnmire (pp. 49–79). Corvallis: Peopling of the Americas Publications, Center for the Study of the First Americans, Oregon State University.

Goodyear, Albert C. 2005. "Evidence of Pre-Clovis Sites in the Eastern United States". In *Paleoamerican Origins: Beyond Clovis*, edited by Robson Bonnichsen, Bradley T. Lepper, Dennis Stanford, and Michael R. Waters (pp. 103–112). College Station: Center for the Study of the First Americans. Texas A&M Press.

Graebner, Norman A. 1945. "The Public Land Policy of the Five Civilized Tribes." *Chronicles of Oklahoma* 23: 107–118.

Gregory, Hiram F. 1977. "Jena Band of Louisiana Choctaw." *American Indian Journal* 3, no. 2: 2–16.

Gremillion, Kristen J. 1996. "The Paleoethnobotanical Record for the Mid-Holocene Southeast." In *Archaeology of the Mid-Holocene Southeast*, edited by Kenneth E. Sassaman and David G. Anderson (pp. 99–114). Gainesville: University of Florida Press.

Halbert, Henry S. 1902. "Bernard Romans' Map of 1772." *Publications of the Mississippi Historical Society* 6: 415–439.

Halligan, Jessi, Michael R. Waters, Angelina Perrotti, Ivy J. Owens, Joshua M. Feinberg, Mark D. Bourne, Brendan Fenerty, et al. 2016.

"Pre-Clovis Occupation 14,550 Years Ago at the Page-Ladson Site, Florida, and The Peopling of the Americas." *Science Advances* 2, no. 5: e1600375. DOI: 10.1126/sciadv.1600375.

Hally, David J., and Robert C. Mainfort Jr. 2004. "Prehistory of the Eastern Interior After 500 BC." In *Handbook of North American Indians*, vol. 14: *Southeast*, edited by Raymond D. Fogelson, (pp. 265–285). Washington, DC: Smithsonian Institution.

Haynes, C. V. 1966. "Elephant Hunting in North America." *Scientific American* 214, no. 6: 104–112.

Haynes. Gary. 2002. *The Early Settlement of North America: The Clovis Era.* New York: Cambridge University Press.

Hill, M. 1981. "Analysis, Synthesis, and Interpretation of the Skeletal Material Excavated for the Gainesville Section of the Tennessee-Tombigbee Waterway." In *Archaeological Investigations of the Gainesville Lake Area of the Tennessee-Tombigbee Waterway*, vol. 4. Tuscaloosa: Office of Archaeological Research report of Investigations 14, University of Alabama.

Hoffecker, John F., Scott A. Elias, and Dennis H. O'Rourke. 2014. "Out of Beringia?" *Science* 343, no. 6174: 979–980.

Hoffecker, John F., W. Roger Powers, and Ted Goebel. 1993. "The Colonization of Beringia and the Peopling of the New World." *Science* 259: 46–53.

Hudson, Charles. 1976. *The Southeastern Indians.* Knoxville: University of Tennessee Press.

Hudson, Charles. 1997. *Knights of Spain, Warriors of the Sun: Hernando De Soto and the South's Ancient Chiefdoms.* Athens: University of Georgia Press.

Hunke, Naomi Ruth. 1986. *B. Frank Belvin: God's Warhorse.* Birmingham, AL: New Hope.

Jackson, Helen Hunt. 1881. *A Century of Dishonor: A Sketch of the United States Government's Dealings with Some of the Indian Tribes.* New York: Harper & Brothers.

Jena Band of Choctaw Indians. 1993. Summary under the Criteria and Evidence for Proposed Finding for Federal Acknowledgment of the Jena Band of Choctaw Indians. U.S. Department of the Interior, Office of Federal Acknowledgement. Available at https://www.bia.gov/sites/bia.gov/files/assets/as-ia/ofa/petition/045_jencht_LA/045_pf.pdf.

Jena Band of Choctaw Indians. 2015. Homepage. Available at www.jenachoctaw.org.

Jenkins, Ned J. 1982. "Archaeology of the Gainesville Lake Area Synthesis." In *Archaeological Investigations of the Gainesville Lake Area of the*

Tennessee-Tombigbee Waterway, vol. 5, Report of Investigations 23. Tuscaloosa: Office of Archaeological Research, University of Alabama.

Jenkins, Ned J., and H. Blaine Ensor. 1982. Gainesville Lake Area Excavations. In *Archaeological Investigations of the Gainesville Lake Area of the Tennessee-Tombigbee Waterway*, vol. 5, Report of Investigations 23. Tuscaloosa: Office of Archaeological Research, University of Alabama.

Jenkins, Ned J., and Richard A. Krause. 1986. *The Tombigbee Watershed in Southeastern Prehistory*. Tuscaloosa: University of Alabama Press.

Jerke, Bud W. 2010. "Cashing in on Capitol Hill: Insider Trading and the Use of Political Intelligence for Profit." *University of Pennsylvania Law Review* 158, no. 5: 1451–1521.

Jones, Nicholas M. 2008/2009. "America Cinches Its Purse Strings on Government Contracts: Navigating Section 8(A) of the Small Business Act through a Recession Economy." *American Indian Law Review* 33, no. 2: 491–523.

Kappler, Charles J. (1904) 1971. *Indian Affairs, Law and Treaties, Vol. 2 (Treaties)*. Washington, DC: Government Printing Office.

Karr, Steven M. 1998/1999. "Now We Have Forgotten the Old Indian Law: Choctaw Culture and the Evolution of Corporal Punishment." *American Indian Law Review* 23, no. 2: 409–423.

Kidwell, Clara Sue. 1995. *Choctaws and Missionaries in Mississippi, 1818–1918*. Norman: University of Oklahoma Press.

Kidwell, Clara Sue. 2004. "Choctaw in the West." In *Handbook of North American Indians*, vol. 14: *Southeast*, edited by Raymond Fogelson (pp. 520–530) Washington, DC: Smithsonian Institution.

Kidwell, Clara Sue. 2008. *The Choctaws in Oklahoma: From Tribe to Nation, 1855–1970*. American Indian Law and Policy Series, no. 2. Norman: University of Oklahoma Press.

Kidwell, Clara Sue, Homer Noley, and George Tinker. 2001. *A Native American Theology*. Mayknoll, NY: Orbis Books.

Kidwell, Clara Sue, and Charles Roberts. 1980. *The Choctaws: A Critical Bibliography*. Bloomington: Indiana University Press.

Kidwell, Clara Sue, and Alan Velie. 2005. *Native American Studies*. Lincoln: University of Nebraska Press.

Kinnaird, Lawrence. 1946. Spain in the Mississippi Valley, 1765–1794. American Historical Association, *Annual Report for 1945*, vol. 2, Washington, DC: Government Printing Office.

Klopotek, Brian. 2011. *Recognition Odysseys: Indigeneity, Race, and Federal Tribal Recognition Policy in Three Louisiana Indian Communities*. Durham, NC: Duke University Press.

Knight, Vernon James. 1998. "Moundville as a Diagrammatic Ceremonial Center." In *Archaeology of the Moundville Chiefdom*, edited by V. J. Knight and Vincas P. Steponaitis (pp. 44–62). Washington, DC: Smithsonian Institution.

Knight, Vernon James, and Vincas P. Steponaitis. 1998. "A New History of Moundville." In *Archaeology of the Moundville Chiefdom*, edited by V. J. Knight and Vincas P. Steponaitis (pp. 1–26). Washington, DC: Smithsonian Institution.

Kotlowski, Dean J. 2002. "Limited Vision: Carl Albert, the Choctaws, and Native American Self-Determination." *American Indian Culture and Research Journal* 26, no. 2: 17–43.

Lambert, Valerie. 2007a. *Choctaw Nation: A Story of American Indian Resurgence.* Lincoln: University of Nebraska Press.

Lambert, Valerie. 2007b. "Political Protest, Conflict, and Tribal Nationalism: The Oklahoma Choctaws and the Termination Crisis of 1959–1970." *American Indian Quarterly* 31, no. 2: 283–309.

Levine, Victoria Lindsay. 2004. "Choctaw at Ardmore, Oklahoma." In *Handbook of North American Indians*, vol. 14: *Southeast*, edited by Raymond Fogelson (pp. 531–533). Washington, DC: Smithsonian Institution.

Lincecum, Gideon. 1904. "Choctaw Traditions About Their Settlement in Mississippi and the Origin of Their Mounds." In *Publications of the Mississippi Historical Society*, vol. 8, edited by Franklin Riley (pp. 521–542). Oxford, Mississippi: Printed for the Mississippi Historical Society.

Lyons, Scott Richard. 2010. *X-Marks: Native Signatures of Assent.* Minneapolis: University of Minnesota Press.

MacPhee, R. D., and P. A. Marks. 1997. "The 40,000 Year Plague: Humans, Hyperdisease, and First-Contact Extinction." In *Natural Change and Human Impact in Madagascar*, edited by S. M. Goodman and B. D. Patterson (pp. 169–217). Washington, DC: Smithsonian Institution.

Martin, Paul S., and Richard G. Klein (eds.) 1984. *Quaternary Extinctions: A Prehistoric Revolution.* Tucson: University of Arizona Press.

Matte, Jacqueline Anderson. 2006. "Extinction by Reclassification: The MOWA Choctaws of South Alabama and Their Struggle for Federal Recognition." *The Alabama Review* 59, no. 3: 163–204.

McKee, Jesse O. 1971. "The Choctaw Indians: A Geographical Study in Cultural Change." *Southern Quarterly* 9: 107–141.

McKee, Jesse O. 1989. *The Choctaw.* Indians of North American series. Langhorne, PA: Chelsea House Publishers.

McKee, Jessie O., and Steve Murray. 1986. "Economic Progress and Development in the Mississippi Band of Choctaw Indians since 1945." In *After*

Removal: The Choctaw in Mississippi, edited by Samuel J. Wells and Rose-anna Tubby (pp. 122–136). Jackson: University Press of Mississippi.

Meltzer, David J. 2002. "What Do You Do When No One's Been There Before? Thoughts on the Exploration and Colonization of New Lands." In *The First Americans: The Pleistocene Colonization of the New World*, edited by N. Jablonski (pp. 25–26). San Francisco: California Academy of Sciences Memoir 27.

Meltzer, David J. 2010. *First Peoples in a New World: Colonizing Ice Age America*. Berkeley: University of California Press.

Meltzer, David J., Donald K. Grayson, Gerardo Ardila, Alex W. Barber, Dena F. Dincausze, C. Vance Haynes, Francisco Mena, Lautaro Nunez and Dennis J. Stanford. 1997. "On the Pleistocene Antiquity of Monte Verde, Southern Chile." *American Antiquity* 62: 659–663.

Milligan, James C. 2003. *The Choctaw of Oklahoma*. Abilene, TX: H.V. Chapman & Sons.

Mississippi Band of Choctaw Indians. 2012. Available at http://www.choctaw.org.

Mississippi Band of Choctaw Indians. 2015. History. Available at http://www.choctaw.org/.

Morse, Dan F., David G. Anderson, and Albert C. Goodyear. 1996. "The Pleistocene-Holocene Transition in the Eastern United States." In *Humans at the End of the Ice Age: The Archaeology of the Pleistocene-Holocene Transition*, edited by Lawrence G. Straus, Bert Eriksen, Jon Erlandson, and David R. Yesner (pp. 319–338). New York: Plenum Press.

Morrison, James D. 1954. "Problems in the Industrial Progress and Development of the Choctaw Nation, 1865 to 1907." *Chronicles of Oklahoma* 32: 70–91.

Nairne, Thomas. (1708) 1988. *Nairne's Muskhogean Journals: The 1708 Expedition to the Mississippi River*. Edited by Alexander Moore. Jackson: University Press of Mississippi.

O'Brien, Greg. 2001. "The Conqueror Meets the Unconquered: Negotiating Cultural Boundaries on the Post-Revolutionary Southern Frontier." *The Journal of Southern History* 67, no. 1: 39–72.

O'Brien, Greg. 2002. *Choctaws in a Revolutionary Age, 1750–1830*. Lincoln: University of Nebraska Press.

O'Brien, Greg. 2008. *Pre-Removal Choctaw History: Exploring New Paths*. Civilization of the American Indian Series, vol. 256. Norman: University of Oklahoma Press.

Office of Federal Acknowledgement. 1997. "Summary Under the Criteria and Evidence for Final Determination against Federal Acknowledgement."

Washington, DC: Office of the Interior. Available at https://www.bia.gov /sites/bia.gov/files/assets/as-ia/ofa/petition/086_mowach_AL/086_fd.pdf.

Okla Chahta Clan of California, Inc. 2018. Homepage. Online document at https://www.oklachahta.org/.

Oklahoma Department of Transportation (ODOT). 2016. "Choctaw Nation of Oklahoma: Economic and Demographic Data. Online document at http://www.odot.org/OK-GOV-DOCS/PROGRAMS-AND -PROJECTS/GRANTS/FASTLANE-US69/Reports-Tech-Info /Tribal%20Data.pdf.

"Oklahoma Indians to Form Company." *The Daily Oklahoman*. November 4, 1917, p. 23.

Osburn, Katherine M. 2007. "'In a Name of Justice and Fairness': The Mississippi Choctaw Indian Federation v. the BIA, 1934." In *Beyond Red Power: Indian Activism in the Twentieth Century*, edited by Dan Cobb and Loretta Fowler (pp. 109–123). Santa Fe, NM: The School for Advanced Research Press.

Osburn, Katherine M. 2016. "Tribal 'Remnants' or State Citizens: Mississippi Choctaws in the Post-Removal South." *American Nineteenth Century History* 17, no. 2: 199–214.

Painter-Thorne, Suzianne D. 2008/2009. "One Step Forward, Two Giant Steps Back: How the 'Existing Indian Family' Exception (Re)Imposes Anglo American Legal Values on American Indian Tribes to the Detriment of Cultural Autonomy. *American Indian Law Review* 33, no. 2: 329–384.

Peebles, Christopher. 1983a. *Excavations in the Lubbub Creek Archaeological Locality: Prehistoric Agricultural Communities in West Central Alabama*, 3 vols. Report on file with the Office of Archaeological Research, Moundville, AL.

Peebles, Christopher. 1983b. "Introduction to Research in the Lubbub Creek Archaeological Locality." In *Excavations in the Lubbub Creek Archaeological Locality: Prehistoric Agricultural Communities in West Central Alabama*, vol. 1, edited by Christopher Peebles (pp. 1–9). Report on file with the Office of Archaeological Research, Moundville, AL.

Peebles, Christopher. 1983c. "Summary and Conclusions: Continuity and Change in a Small Mississippian Community." In *Excavations in the Lubbub Creek Archaeological Locality: Prehistoric Agricultural Communities in West Central Alabama*, vol. 1, edited by Christopher Peebles (pp. 394–407). Report on file with the Office of Archaeological Research, Moundville, AL.

Peebles, Christopher. 1986. "Paradise Lost, Strayed, and Stolen: Prehistoric Social Devolution in the Southeast." In *The Burden of Being Civilized: An Anthropological Perspective on the Discontents of Civilization*, edited by M. Richardson and M. C. Webb (pp. 24–40). Southern Anthropological Society Proceedings. Athens: University of Georgia Press.

Peebles, Christopher. 1987. "The Rise and Fall of the Mississippian in Western Alabama: The Moundville and Summerville Phases, A.D. 1000 to 1600." *Mississippi Archaeology* 22: 1–31.

Peebles, Christopher, and Cyrill B. Mann. 1983. "Culture and Chronology in the Lubbub Creek Archaeological Locality." In *Excavations in the Lubbub Creek Archaeological Locality: Prehistoric Agricultural Communities in West Central Alabama*, vol. 1, edited by Christopher Peebles (pp. 64–78). Report on file with the Office of Archaeological Research, Moundville, AL.

Perdue, Theda. 1988. "Indians in Southern History." In *Indians in American History*, edited by Frederick E. Hoxie (pp. 137–159). Arlington Heights, IL: Harlan Davidson.

Pesantubbee, Michelene. 1999. "Beyond Domesticity: Choctaw Women Negotiating the Tension Between Choctaw Culture and Protestantism." *Journal of the American Academy of Religion* 67, no. 2: 387–410.

Pesantubbee, Michelene. 2005. *Choctaw Women in a Chaotic World: The Clash of Cultures in the Colonial Southeast*. Albuquerque: University of New Mexico Press.

Peterson, John H. Jr. 1972. "Assimilation, Separation, and Out-Migration in an American Indian Group." *American Anthropologist* 74: 1286–1295.

Peterson, John H. Jr. 1987. "The Mississippi Choctaws: A Pattern of Persistence." In *Persistence of Pattern in Mississippi Culture*. Mississippi Department of Archives and History, pp. 3–9. Jackson, MS.

Peterson, John H., Jr. 1992. "Choctaw Self-Determination in the 1980s." In *Indians of the Southeastern United States in the Late 20th Century*, edited by J. Anthony Paredes (pp. 140–161). Tuscaloosa: University of Alabama.

Purdy, Barbara. 1992. "Florida's Archaeological Wet Sites." In the *Wetland Revolution in Prehistory*, edited by Bryony Coles (pp. 113–124). Proceedings of a conference held by the Prehistory Society and WARP at the University of Exeter, April 1991.

Rangel, Rodrigo. (ca. 1540) 1993. "Account of the Northern Conquest and Discovery of Hernando De Soto." In *The De Soto Chronicles: The Expedition of Hernando De Soto to North America in 1539–1543*, vols. 1 & 2, edited by Lawrence A. Clayton, Vernon J. Knight Jr., and Edward C. Moore. Tuscaloosa: University of Alabama Press.

Riley, Lorinda. 2014/2015. "When a Tribal Entity Becomes a Nation: The Role of Politics in the Shifting Federal Recognition Regulations." *American Indian Law Review* 39, no. 2: 451–505.

Roberts, Charles. 1986. "The Second Choctaw Removal, 1903." In *After Removal: The Choctaw in Mississippi*, edited by Samuel J. Wells and Roseanna Tubby (pp. 94–111). Jackson: University Press of Mississippi.

Rockwell, Stephen J. 2010. *Indian Affairs and the Administrative State in the Nineteenth Century.* Cambridge: Cambridge University Press.

Romans, Bernard. (1775) 1999. *A Concise Natural History of East and West Florida*, edited by Kathryn Holland Braund. Tuscaloosa: University of Alabama Press.

Sassaman, Kenneth E., and David G. Anderson. 2004. "Late Holocene period, 3750 to 650 BC." In *Handbook of North American Indians*, vol. 14: *Southeast*, edited by Raymond D. Fogelson (pp. 101–114). Washington, DC: Smithsonian Institution.

Satz, Ronald N. 1986. "The Mississippi Choctaw: From the Removal Treaty to the Federal Agency." In *After Removal: The Choctaw in Mississippi*, edited by Samuel J. Wells and Roseanna Tubby (pp. 3–32). Jackson: University Press of Mississippi.

Scarry, C. Margaret. 1998. "Domestic Life on the Northwest Riverbank at Moundville." In *Archaeology of the Moundville Chiefdom*, edited by V. J. Knight and Vincas P. Steponaitis (pp. 63–101). Washington, DC: Smithsonian Institution.

Schoeninger, Margaret J., and Mark C. Schurr. 1998. "Human Subsistence at Moundville: The Stable-Isotope Data." In *Archaeology of the Moundville Chiefdom*, edited by V. J. Knight and Vincas P. Steponaitis (pp. 120–132). Washington, DC: Smithsonian Institution.

Schuldenrein, Joseph. 1996. "Geoarchaeology and the Mmid-Holocene Landscape History of the Greater Southeast." In *Archaeology of the Mid-Holocene Southeast*, edited by Kenneth E. Sassaman and David G. Anderson (pp. 3–27). Gainesville: University of Florida Press.

Scott, Susan L. 1983. "Analysis, Synthesis and Interpretation of Faunal Remains from the Lubbub Creek Archaeological Locality." In *Prehistoric Agricultural Communities in West Central Alabama: Studies of Material Remains from the Lubbub Creek Archaeological Locality*, vol. 2, edited by Christopher Peebles (pp. 272–379). University of Michigan. Report submitted to the U.S. Army Corps of Engineers, Mobile District.

Scribner, John C.L., BG. n.d. *Choctaw Indian Code Talkers of World War I.* Texas Military Forces Museum, Austin, TX. Available at http://www.texasmilitaryforcesmuseum.org/choctaw/codetalkers.htm.

Sheehan, Bernard. 1974. *Seeds of extinction: Jeffersonian philanthropy and the American Indian*. New York: W.W. Norton.

Smith, Bruce D. 1978. *Mississippian Settlement Patterns*. New York: Academic Press.

Smith, Bruce D. 1986. "The Archaeology of the Southeastern United States: From Dalton to De Soto, 10,500–500 B.P." In *Advances in World Archaeology*, vol. 5, edited by F. Wendorf and A. Close (pp. 1–92). Orlando, FL: Academic Press.

Smith, Bruce D., and C. Wesley Cowan. 1987. "Domesticated *Chenopodium* in Prehistoric Eastern North America: New Accelerator Dates from Eastern Kentucky." *American Antiquity* 52: 355–357.

Sonneborn, Liz. 2007. *The Choctaws*. Minneapolis, MN: Lerner.

Spoehr, Alexander, 1947. *Changing Kinship Systems: A Study in the Acculturation of the Creeks, Cherokee, and Choctaw*. Chicago, IL: Field Museum of Natural History.

Spring, Ryan. 2011. "Choctaw Nation and the American Civil War." Iti Fabvussa, *Biskinik*, October 2011. Available at https://www.choctawnation.com/sites/default/files/2015/10/14/2011.10_Choctaw_Nation_and_the_American_Civil_War.pdf.

Stanford, Dennis. 1991. "Clovis Origins and Adaptations: An Introductory Perspective." In *Clovis Origins and Adaptations*, edited by Robson Bonnichsen and Karen L. Turnmire (pp. 1–14). Corvallis: Center for the Study of the First Americans, Oregon State University.

Steponaitis, Vincas P. 1998. "Population Trends at Moundville." In *Archaeology of the Moundville Chiefdom*, edited by V. J. Knight and Vincas P. Steponaitis (pp. 26–44). Washington, DC: Smithsonian Institution.

Strong, Pauline T., and Barrik Van Winkle. 1993. "Tribe and Nation: American Indians and American Nationalism." *Social Analysis: The International Journal of Social and Cultural Practice*, No. 33, Nations, Colonies and Metropoles, pp. 9–26.

Strout, Benjamin. 1982. "A New Era." In *Tribal Government: A New Era*, edited by William Brescia (pp. 19–44). Philadelphia, MS: Choctaw Heritage Press, Mississippi Band of Choctaw Indians.

Swanton, John R. 1911. "Indian Tribes of the Lower Mississippi Valley and Adjacent Coast of the Gulf of Mexico." *Bureau of American Ethnology Bulletin*, No. 43. Washington, DC: Government Printing Office.

Swanton, John R. 1918. "An early account of the Choctaw Indians." *American Anthropological Association* 5, no 2: 51–72.

Swanton, John R. 1946. "The Indians of the Southeastern United States." *Bureau of American Ethnology Bulletin* 137. Washington, DC: Government Printing Office.

Swanton, John R. (1931) 2001. *Source Material for the Social and Ceremonial Life of the Choctaw Indians.* Reprint. Tuscaloosa: University of Alabama Press.

Thompson, Ian. 2008. "'*Chahta Intikba Im Aiikhvna*': Learning from the Choctaw Ancestors: Integrating Indigenous and Experimental Approaches in the Study of Mississippian Technology." Unpublished PhD dissertation, Albuquerque, University of New Mexico.

U.S. Census Bureau. 2018a. "My Tribal Area." Available at https://www .census.gov/tribal/?aianihh=2300.

U.S. Census Bureau. 2018b. "Quick Facts." Available at https://www.census .gov/quickfacts/ms.

Unser, Daniel H. 1988. "Economic Relations in the Southeast Until 1783." In *Handbook of North American Indians*, vol. 4, *History of Indian-White Relations*, edited by Wilcomb E. Washburn (pp. 391–95). Washington, DC: Smithsonian Institute Scholarly Press.

Watkins, Joe. 2018. "Indian New Deal, 1934–1941." The American Mosaic. Available at The American Indian Experience, ABC-CLIO, https:// americanindian.abc-clio.com/Topics/Display/23.

Webb, Thompson, Patrick J. Bartlein, Sany P. Harrison, and Katherine H. Anderson. 1993. "Vegetation, Lake Levels, and Climate in Eastern North America for the Past 18,000 Years." In *Global Climate Since the Last Glacial Maximum*, edited by H. E. Wright Jr., J. E. Kutzbach. T. Webb III, W. E. Ruddiman. F. A. Street-Perrott, and P. J. Bartlein (pp. 415–467). Minneapolis: University of Minneapolis Press.

Welch, Paul D. 1991. *Moundville's Economy.* Tuscaloosa: University of Alabama Press.

Welch, Paul D. 1998. "Outlying Sites within the Moundville Chiefdom." In *Archaeology of the Moundville Chiefdom*, edited by V. J. Knight and Vincas P. Steponaitis (pp. 133–166). Washington, DC: Smithsonian Institution.

Welch, Paul D., and C. Margaret Scarry. 1995. "Status-Related Variation in Foodways in the Moundville Chiefdom." *American Antiquity* 60: 397–419.

Wells, Samuel J. 1982. "Treaties and the Choctaw People." In *Tribal Government: A New Era*, edited by William Brescia (pp. 14–18). Philadelphia, MS: Choctaw Heritage Press, Mississippi Band of Choctaw Indians.

Whicker, J. Wesley. 1922. Tecumseh and Pushmataha. *Indiana Magazine of History* 18, no. 4: 315–331.

White, Lonnie. 1979. "Indian Soldiers of the 36th Division." *Military History of Texas and the Southwest* 15: 7–20.

Wilson, Michael Clayton, and James A. Burnes. 1999. "Searching for the Earliest Canadians: Wide Corridors, Narrow Doors, Small Windows." In *Ice Age People of North America: Environments, Origins, and Adaptations,* edited by Robson Bonnichsen and Karen L. Turnmire (pp. 213–248). Corvallis: Oregon State University Press.

Wise, Jennings Cropper. 1931. Edited, revised, and with an Introduction by Vine Deloria, Jr. 1971. *The Red Man in the New World Drama: A Politico-Legal Study, with a Pageantry of American Indian History.* New York: MacMillan.

Wolfe, Cheri L. 1987. "'Something Tells Me This Feeling about the Land Is the Old Choctaw Religion': The Persistence of Choctaw Culture in Mississippi since 1830." In *Persistence of Pattern in Mississippi Culture,* edited by Patty C. Black (pp. 10–27). Jackson: Mississippi Department of Archives and History.

Woods, Patricia D. 1978. "The Relations Between the French of Colonial Louisiana and the Choctaw, Chickasaw and Natchez Indians, 1699–1762." PhD diss., Louisiana State University and Agricultural and Mechanical College. LSU Historical Dissertations and Theses. 3307.

Wright, Muriel H. 1923. *The Story of Oklahoma.* Oklahoma City: Webb Publishing Company.

Wright, Muriel H. 1929. *The Oklahoma History.* Guthrie, OK: Co-operative Publishing.

Wright, Muriel H. 1939. *Our Oklahoma.* Guthrie, OK: Co-operative Publishing Company.

Wright, Muriel H. 1951. *A Guide to the Indian Tribes of Oklahoma.* Civilization of the American Indian series, Vol. 33, Norman: University of Oklahoma Press.

Wright, Muriel H. George H. Shirk, and Kenny A. Franks. 1976. *Mark of Heritage: Oklahoma Historical Markers.* Oklahoma City: Oklahoma Historical Society.

Wright, Muriel H., and Joseph Thoburn. 1929. *Oklahoma: A History of the State and its People.* New York: Lewis Historical Publishing.

Young, Mary E. 1958. "Indian Removal and Land Allotment: The Civilized Tribes and Jacksonian Justice." *The American Historical Review* 64, no. 1: 31–45.

Further Readings

Bowmar, Lt. Joseph. (1804) 2006. "Letter to William C. C. Claiborne." In *The Territorial Papers of the United States: The Territory of Orleans, 1803–1812*, edited by Clarence E. Carter. Buffalo, NY: W.S. Hein.

Britten, Thomas A. 1997. *American Indians in World War I: At Home and at War.* Albuquerque, NM: University of New Mexico Press.

Clark, Daniel. 1803. Letter to Secretary of State James Madison. In *The Territorial Papers of the United States: The Territory of Orleans, 1803–1812*, edited by Clarence E. Carter, vol. 9 (pp. 62–64). Washington, DC: Government Printing Office.

Collier, Peter. 2006. *Medal of Honor: Portraits of Valor Beyond the Call of Duty.* New York: Artisan Press.

Collins, Michael B. 1999. *Clovis Blade Technology: A Comparative Study of the Kevin Davis Cache.* Texas. Austin, TX: University of Texas Press.

Fogelson, Raymond D. 2001. "Foreword." In *Anthropologists and Indians in the New South*, edited by Rachel A. Bonney and J. Anthony Paredes (pp. ix–xi). Tuscaloosa: University of Alabama Press.

Fogelson, Raymond D. 2004. History of Archaeological Research. In *Handbook of North American Indians*, vol. 14: *Southeast*, edited by Raymond Fogelson. pp. 499–519. Washington, DC: Smithsonian Institution.

Gardner, Reginald. 1983. Choctaw Self-Determination: an Overview. In *Choctaw Anthology*, edited by Jane Anderson, pp. 55–59. Philadelphia, PA: Choctaw Heritage Press, Mississippi Band of Choctaw Indians.

Katz, Lienke. 1996. *The History of Blackwater Draw*. Corrales, NM: Eastern New Mexico University Printing Services.

Pushmataha. 1819. Speech. *American State Papers: Indian Affairs* 2: 230.

Rouquette, Dominique. 1938. *The Choctaw*. Translated by Olivia Blanchard. Survey of Federal Archives, New Orleans.

Shott, Michael J. 1997. Stones and Shafts Redux: The Metric Discrimination of Chipped-Stone Dart and Arrow Points. *American Antiquity* 62: 86–101.

Sibley, John. 1805. Historical Sketches of the Several Indian Tribes of Louisiana, South of the Arkansas River, and between the Mississippi and River Grand. *American State Papers: Indian Affairs* 1: 721–725.

U.S. Census Bureau 2018a "My Tribal Area." Available at https://www .census.gov/tribal/?aianihh=2300.

U.S. Census Bureau 2018b "Quick Facts." Available at https://www.census .gov/quickfacts/ms.

Waters, Michael R., Charlotte D. Pevny, and David L. Carlson. 2011. *Clovis Lithic Technology: Investigation of a Stratified Workshop at the Gault Site, Texas*. College Station, TX: Peopling of the Americas Publication, Texas A&M.

Watt, Marilyn J. 1986. "Federal Indian Policy and Tribal Development in Louisiana: The Jena Band of Choctaw." Unpublished PhD diss. State College: Pennsylvania State University.

Wells, Samuel J., and Roseanna Tubby, eds. 1986. *After Removal: The Choctaw in Mississippi*. Jackson, MS: University Press of Mississippi.

Wright, Muriel H. 1928. The Removal of the Choctaw to the Indian Territory, 1830–1833. *Chronicles of Oklahoma* 6: 103–128.

Index

Note: Page numbers in *italics* indicate illustrations.

About the Author

Joe E. Watkins, PhD, is a member of the Choctaw Nation of Oklahoma. He is author of *Indigenous Archaeology: American Indian Values and Scientific Perspectives* (2000) and *Sacred Sites and Repatriation* (2005), and coauthor with Carol Ellick of *The Anthropology Graduate's Guide: From Student to a Career* (2011). He was the American Indian Liaison Officer and Chief of the Tribal Relations and American Cultures program of the National Park Service from 2013–2018, director of the Native American Studies program at the University of Oklahoma from 2006 to 2013, and associate professor of anthropology at the University of New Mexico prior to that.